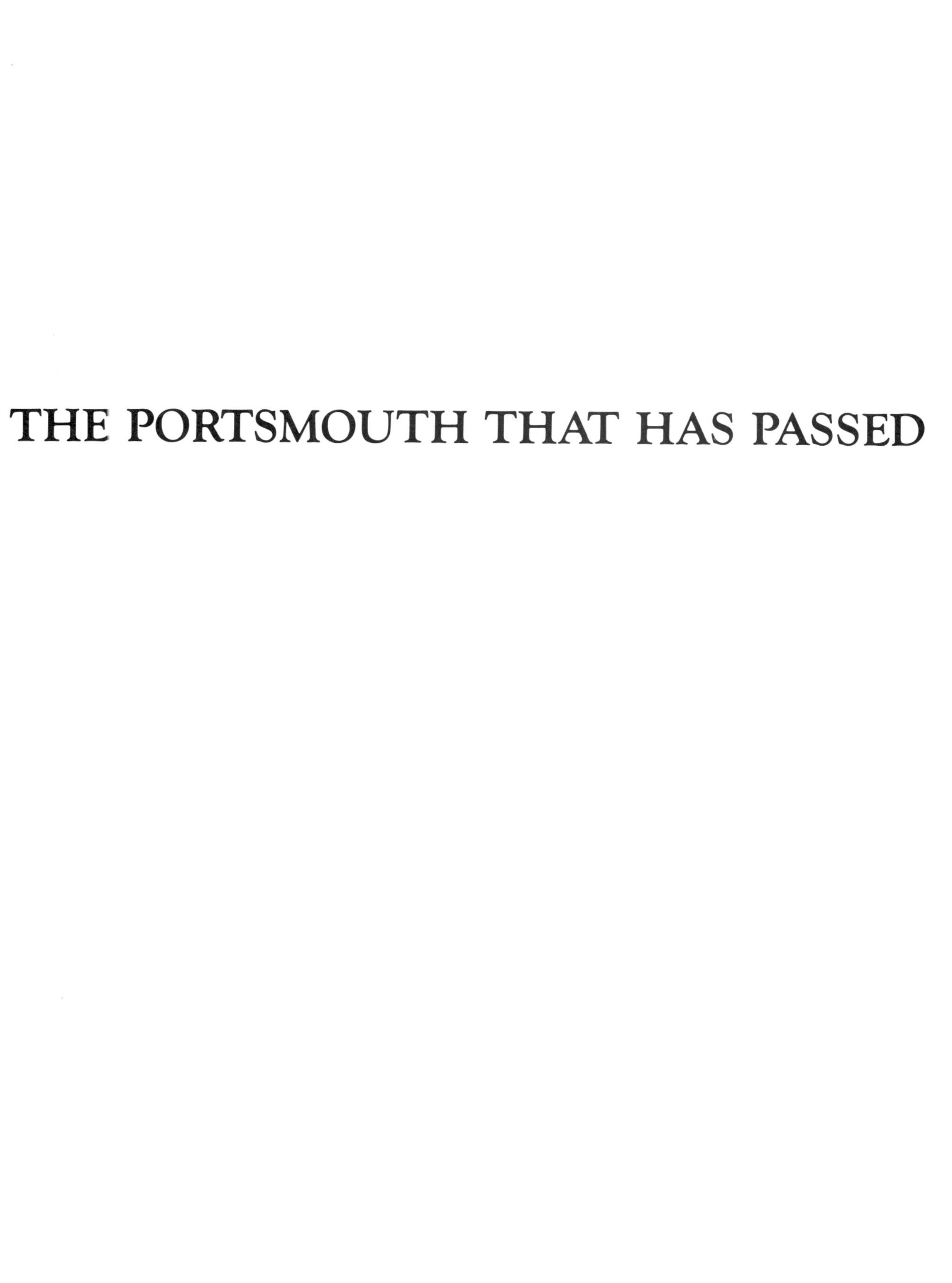

THE PORTSMOUTH THAT HAS PASSED

W.G. Gates

The Portsmouth That Has Passed

A Panorama of a Thousand Years

William G. Gates
Edited by
Nigel Peake

Published by Milestone Publications
62 Murray Road, Horndean
Portsmouth, Hants PO8 9JL

In conjunction with
The News
Hilsea, Portsmouth

Typeset by Barbara James, Hayling Island

Printed and Bound in Great Britain by
R.J. Acford, Industrial Estate, Chichester, Sussex

British Library Cataloguing in Publication Data

Gates, W.G.
The Portsmouth that has passed : with a glimpse of Gosport.—2nd ed.
1. Portsmouth (Hampshire)—History
I. Title II. Peake, Nigel III. Gates, W.G.
942.2'792 DA690.P8

ISBN 1-85265-111-3

Foreword

by

Councillor F.A.J. Emery-Wallis, F.S.A., Leader of Hampshire County Council

The Crimean War was in its final stages when W.G. Gates was born in 1856. He arrived in Portsmouth six years later and, after service in the Royal Navy, he became a cub reporter with the Evening News. *A History of Naval Ships* was his first book and in 1899, to commemorate its centenary, the Hampshire Telegraph published his illustrated *History of Portsmouth.* Until his death he was to write continuously of the city's eventful history.

We were to meet because I started to collect books on Portsmouth. My first purchase was an early edition of Marryat's *Peter Simple — The Ancient and Modern History of Portsmouth*, published in 1800; it cost me, or my parents, 7s.6d. It was a beautiful copy and I have it still. My collecting continued throughout the war and in one school holiday my father took me to meet a friend who was also interested in Portsmouth history; it was W.G. as he was always known. Then in his eighties, he used to speak about the place he had known just as if it was the narrative of one of his histories. It was fascinating to listen to a man who, before I was born, had retired after being Editor of the Evening News and the Hampshire Telegraph for some 50 years. His first recollections were those of a Portsmouth where the town walls were still in place, with access only by drawbridge and through gates. When he returned in 1877 "vast changes had taken place. The ramparts and moats had disappeared, the town was drained and compulsory education was providing many new schools". Throughout his career his influence for progress was often critical and he obviously had great pride in the transformation he had seen of the city's health, housing and education services. He was equally determined that he would do one last thing for Portsmouth and that was to provide a reminder of its colourful history at a time when its inhabitants would be struggling to rebuild a city devastated by a war which had swept away much of the legacy from past times. He was determined to complete his new history to be called *The Portsmouth That Has Passed.* It was a difficult undertaking: the museums were closed, their collections destroyed, many of the Central Library's local books had been sent to the country; George Seaford's splendid bookshop, with his incomparable collection of Portsmouth books totally destroyed, as was Harry Moth's printing works in the High Street together with the Charpentier collection of illustrations.

W.G. was himself now very fragile and confined to his house in Drayton but his friends at the Evening News were always ready to help. My task was to help track down essential illustrations. The last request came in a letter the week before I left for National Service in June, 1945. It was accompanied by a copy of his first work on Portsmouth, his story of the Free Mart Fair. The following spring my parents wrote to me in Alexandria to say that he had died aged 90. His testament to the city which he wrote in 1927 is almost identical to that of 1945: "A city with wide avenues, bordered by stately trees, with parks and gardens open to all and an honoured age free from want and fear".

This new edition of 1987 can act as a spur that a vision is still required.

Freddie Emery-Wallis

ACKNOWLEDGEMENTS

I thank Mrs. Dorothy Gates, daughter-in-law of the late W.G. Gates, for her help in providing material for this updated version and also for the photograph of the author on page 2.

Sketches taken from the original book came from the collection of Messrs. Charpentier Ltd., formerly of High Street, Portsmouth.

Photographs of the municipal silver on pages 22, 27 and 88 appear by courtesy of Portsmouth City Council.

Introduction

Few people knew or cared for Portsmouth as deeply as W.G. Gates. His books on the area stand as a lasting tribute to its colourful and crowded history, and his journalistic enthusiasm for telling that story continued long after his official retirement. When he died at the age of 90, he was still busy on *The Portsmouth That Has Passed,* a task that was completed by his colleague F.J.H. Young. The first edition, published in 1946, was a condensed version of his huge and impressive *History of Portsmouth,* originally published in 1899 by the Evening News and Hampshire Telegraph Company. The story ended with the outbreak of the second world war, a grievous time in which large areas of the city which Gates loved were laid waste by enemy bombers.

Since then, there have been numerous calls to re-publish the work, and this book is a response to that interest. W.G.'s original text, with his various asides and typical comments, has been retained, but I have taken the liberty of adding explanatory footnotes where applicable. From 1939 onwards, I have updated the story in a way of which I hope "the Chief" would have approved, and which I trust retains the flavour of the original.

There will inevitably be omissions, for which I apologise, but Portsmouth's story is far more eventful than most, and even journalists accustomed to condensing their work find difficulty in cramming 1,000 years into 200 pages. To those who wish to follow it further, I can do no better than to recommend W.G. Gates's *History of Portsmouth,* of which the Portsmouth Central Library's Local History Collection has copies. There is also the impressive "Portsmouth Papers" series, published by the City Council, and a host of books slim and fat, old and new, devoted to the subject.

Nigel Peake
1987

Portsmouth is Born

491 B.C.

Although the early history of Portchester is uncertain, the town was undoubtedly the Mother of Portsmouth. According to Higden, the Monk of Chester, Peres and his elder brother Ferrex, sons of an ancient British king, fought for the crown and Ferrex was slain. Peres then built Caer-Peris, by which name Portchester became known to the Britons. This event is said to have happened about 491 B.C.

In connection with this subject, it is interesting to note that at Portchester the spot is pointed out where Vespasian is said to have embarked for the siege of Jerusalem, and not far distant a clump of trees on the seashore is said to indicate where St Paul landed in Britain. It is known as Paulsgrove to this day. These traditions, however, have no claim to be regarded as serious history.

These highly fanciful references in the second paragraph are doubtless due to the fact that as a journalist, W.G. Gates would have found them irresistible.

A Roman Revolt

286 A.D.

The first reference to Portsmouth as a naval station carries us back to the year 286, when a sea captain named Carausius, who had been sent by Rome to suppress piracy, became a master pirate himself. He assumed Imperial power and even had his own coinage minted. He was eventually killed by a rival, and then Rome sent a great force to crush the rebellion. This was accomplished, and then, realising the commanding position of Portchester, the Romans developed it as a naval station.

Gates records that shortly before his book was originally published, one of Carausius's gold coins was sold for £200. At about the same time, two skeletons were found at Portchester, and in the skull of each were Roman coins. These had been placed beneath the tongue, in accordance with tradition, to pay old Charon to ferry them across the Styx.

The Mystery of Lumps Mill

310 A.D.

The discovery of broken pottery in Lumps Lane and also in the nearby cemetery has been the subject of much conjecture among antiquarians, and the opinion of one authority is that the place may have been used for depositing the urns which contained the ashes of the dead. So mingles the dust of far separated generations — ancient Roman and modern Englishman lie sleeping together.

According to an ancient deed, the origin of this name can be traced to an early possessor of land in the vicinity. One Philip, son of Peter de Esteneye, "hels one acre of land at Esteneye, under Ralph Lumpee." The name appears on a map of 1660, being then applied to a farm situated behind what is now Lumps Fort and extending beyond what was formerly known as Lumps Lane.

Roman Treasure at Southsea

310 A.D.

Not many traces have been found of the presence of Romans in Portsea Island, but a few years ago some workmen employed by Mr. H. Evans, in preparing the foundations of a new house at the upper end of what was then known as Lumps Lane, unearthed some broken pottery which had apparently formed part of burial urns. Then came a great surprise. By accident, one of the workmen pierced a complete urn and in it was found nearly a thousand Roman coins. Many were selected for the National Collection, others were generously distributed by Mr. Evans to the local museum and personal friends, including the writer. It has been reasonably suggested that the money had been hidden by an officer who had been ordered to Rome and never returned to recover his treasure, which he may have meant to share with some beauteous British maiden.

The Battle of Longborth

501 A.D.

The earliest mention of Portsmouth is in the Saxon Chronicle. We are there told that in the year 501 a body of Saxons landed here from two large galleys, defeated the Britons drawn up to oppose them, killed their commander and took possession of the adjacent country. Dr. Turner, in his *History of the Anglo-Saxons*, quotes the description by a Welsh poet who was present at a fight which may well have been the conflict referred to. It took place at Longborth, which means The Haven of Ships, and was some harbour on the South Coast. In 1816, some workmen on the top of Portsdown opened two ancient barrows, in which they found the remains of twelve men who had evidently been slain in battle, as the iron tip of a spear was in the skull of one and a spear-head by the side of another.

Some later historians have cast doubt on this incident. The Chronicle refers to a landing "in this place which is called Portes mutha" but some researchers say this could have been anywhere on the South Coast. They prefer the theory that Portsmouth took its name from the Romans' Portchester, which was known as Portus Adurni — the mouth of the port.

The British Navy is Born

897

This year, with a fleet of his own design, King Alfred the Great, in the waters of the Solent, gained a complete victory over the Danes and later in the year captured 20 of their ships in the Channel. From that far-off day, Portsmouth with Gosport has been the chief home of the Navy upon which "under the good providence of God our wealth, prosperity and peace depend."

Mystery of a Missing Charter

1106

Although no Charter has been found of earlier date than 1194, there is reason to believe that one was granted by King Henry the First in 1106 under the title of "Approved Men of Portsmouth," and that it was surrendered to King Richard the First in 1194 for a new Charter — at a price, for he was much in need of money at the time.

Certainly, Richard was in dire need of money to finance various revenge actions against France and Austria. As he gathered his fleet — and his purses — at Portsmouth, the astute leading citizens doubtless saw this as a golden opportunity to press for a charter which allowed them an annual fair and exempted them from various taxes.

The King founded a Priory

1133

The last expedition into Normandy by King Henry I is remarkable because of an eclipse of the sun and a subterranean disturbance just as he was about to embark. One who was present writes: "Whilst the King was waiting, there suddenly appeared clouds in the sky of such magnitude as had never been seen before in England. The King and his attendants, astonished at this sudden darkness, looking towards the sun saw it appear like a new moon. Several stars appeared, and while the ships were ready to receive the King, the sea being calm and only a gentle breeze of wind, the large anchors of one of the ships were suddenly moved by some unseen cause out of the ground, so that she drove against the next, to the astonishment of all that beheld it, and notwithstanding all their endeavours to prevent it, eight ships were dashed together so that nothing whole of them remained." The King, in gratitude for his deliverance, founded a church at Portchester which he dedicated to the Virgin Mary.

The First Church of St Mary

1170

For the safety of his soul, Baldwin de Portesia "gave and granted to the Church of St Mary at Southwick in free, pure and perpetual alms the church of Portsea with the land and tithes and all things belonging to it, with half a hide of land in Stubinton and pasture for 100 sheep, 15 beasts and 50 hogs in common with his men."

This was the first church devoted to Christian worship on the Island of Portsea. With little alteration, except the provision of an outside stairway to the gallery and a square tower at the west front, the church survived until the middle of the last century. It had no pretensions to architectural beauty, but age rendered it picturesque and many hallowed associations endeared it to the people.

The Church of the Navy

1180

This year, John de Gisors granted to the Canons of Southwick "for the repose of my soul and the souls of my father and mother and of my ancestors and of my heirs, a certain place to erect thereon a chapel in honour of the glorious martyr Thomas, Archbishop of Canterbury, on my land which is called Sudwede in the Isle of Portesia."

Such was the beginning of the church of St Thomas, where thousands of men who helped to make England great, pledged their faith, their hope and their willing service at the foot of the High Altar. The ancient church is now encompassed by massive Cathedral walls, much to the regret of many Portsmouth families who preferred their church as they and their ancestors knew and loved it.

This church, originally dedicated to the then newly-martyred St Thomas a Becket, became the city's Anglican Cathedral in 1927 — a date when it obviously fell out of favour with Gates and other older residents. Nearer our own time, their misgivings have been echoed by others whenever plans have been submitted to extend the building.

What Manner of Town was it?

1182

As already recorded, King Alfred the Great started the Navy here in 897. In 957 King Edgar formed the first Channel fleet which had Portsmouth as its principal base. In 1066, King Harold fitted out a fleet of 700 ships, which cruised in the Solent until false news caused its dispersal and William the Conqueror landed at Pevensey. Twenty years later, William the First was here to oppose Canute IV. In 1101 Robert, Duke of Normandy, landed here with a powerful force. In 1106, Portsmouth received its first Charter from Henry I. In 1123 the King spent his Whitsuntide here. In 1133 the Empress Matilda, daughter of Henry I, landed here with a small force to assert her right to the Throne. In 1174 Henry II embarked, taking with him as prisoner William the Lion, King of Scotland. In 1175 King Henry returned with his victorious army from Normandy. In 1182 Henry II before his departure for France "made his Will by the seaside at Portsmouth." This was the king who set about the rebuilding of Portchester Castle. And so the record runs with ever increasing importance, and it may be justly claimed that Portsmouth has occupied a most important place in the life of the nation for a thousand years.

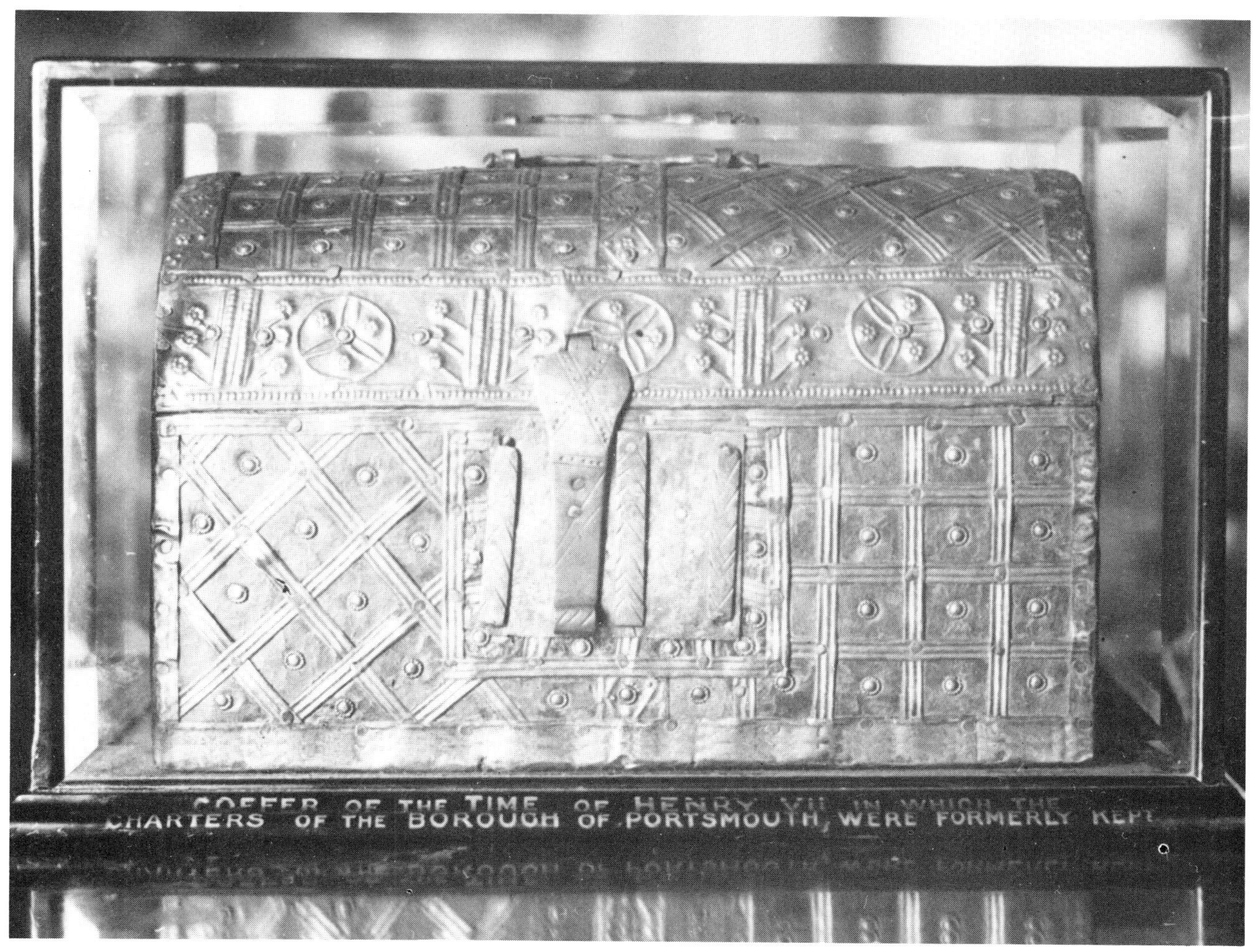

Portsmouth receives a new Charter

1194

In the spring of this year, King Richard I assembled here a large fleet for an expedition to France. He was so anxious to put to sea that he set sail in a gale of wind, but was obliged to take shelter in the Isle of Wight, whence he returned to Portsmouth. It was on May 12th that he finally embarked and the fleet set sail. During his residence here, he did not fail to recognise the great importance of the port and took counsel with the leading inhabitants concerning its development. He granted a new Charter which authorised the holding of an annual fair, a Free Mart, and other privileges. He also gave orders for houses to be built, and also a King's Hall with chapel attached. This hall must have been of fair proportions, as it is on record that King John and his Queen Isabella feasted and made merry there during Whitsuntide in 1201. The hall was at the upper end of the thoroughfare that was later named St Nicholas Street. For the safe keeping of the new Charter, the Corporation caused a casket to be made which is now unique and above price.

The Free Mart Fair originally lasted 15 days, and all visitors (foreigners included) were exempted from all the usual taxes and tolls for this period, as well as from arrest for debt.

The Hospital of St Nicholas

1212

Over 700 years ago the first hospital was established in Portsmouth and for three centuries it ministered not only to the bodily but also to the spiritual needs of the sick, the poor and the suffering. The Domus Dei or Hospital of St Nicholas (Patron Saint of Sailors) was established by Peter de Rupibus, Bishop of Winchester, in 1212. Of its history until its abolition in 1540, little is known, but it attracted the generous attention of the faithful and its endowments included "a certain land called Westwode," given by Charter by the Burgesses of Portsmouth. At the time of the dissolution of the monasteries in 1540, the buildings and revenues were surrendered to the King by the Master, John Incent, who, two days later, was rewarded with a Deanery of St Paul's.

The Bishop of Winchester referred to was also known as Pierre des Roches. The subsequent history of the Domus Dei is a particularly chequered one. Used as an armoury from 1540 for two decades, it then became the military governor's residence, although the chapel was retained for religious use. Charles II married his Portuguese bride Catherine de Braganza there in 1662. Two centuries of decline and disrepair followed until the chapel was restored in 1867 to become the Garrison Church. It was reduced to a burnt-out shell during one of Portsmouth's worst second world war air raids, on January 10th, 1941, and stands today as a silent memorial.

King John's Historic Order

1212

On May 20th, King John issued the following order to the Sheriff of Southampton: "We order you, without delay, to cause our Docks at Portsmouth to be enclosed with a good and strong wall for the preservation of our ships and galleys, and likewise to cause penthouses to be made to the same walls in which all our ships' tackle may be safely kept. Use as much despatch as you can lest in the ensuing winter our ships and galleys should suffer any damage by your default. When we know the cost it shall be accounted to you."

This order has been held to indicate the origin of Portsmouth Dockyard, but in effect it proves the existence of the Docks before 1212, otherwise there would have been no necessity to enclose them "with a good and strong wall."

Southsea Common — A Military Rendezvous

1221

Although Portsmouth's chief claim to fame is as the home of the Navy, it has also for several hundred years served as a great military rendezvous. In 1194, King Richard assembled here a strong body of troops, with whom he sailed for Barfleur; in 1221, Henry III assembled here one of the finest armies ever raised in England; in 1253, the King, with troops and a thousand transports, sailed for France; in 1346, Edward III assembled here an army of more than 30,000 men; in 1386, the Duke of Lancaster embarked with an army of 28,000 men; in 1475, the King reviewed 30,000 men on Southsea Common; in 1545, King Henry VIII was here with his military forces; and from that time through the centuries Portsmouth has never been without a military garrison.

The last few words were true in Gates' time, but the Portsmouth Garrison was officially closed in 1960. All that remains today of the military presence is a skeleton force at the Royal Marines Barracks at Eastney.

Hospital of the Magdalene

1254

Seven hundred years ago on the main road to Portsmouth, there was a small refuge for pilgrims, tired wayfarers, the sick, and lepers. There is not much historical reference to it, but the fact that the monks were authorised to collect alms is an indication of its good work, which continued until the dissolution of the monasteries. It is on record that the monks found pleasure in maintaining a large colony of white swans upon the two extensive ponds in the vicinity, one in what is now the Guildhall Square. Was it spiritual inspiration or mere coincidence which led the Guardians of the Poor to choose for their Home of Public Assistance the very site of the ancient Hospital of the Magdalene?

The memory of the monks' swans lives on in the name of White Swan Road, which runs off Guildhall Walk, and of course the White Swan public house on its corner.

Seals of the City

1304

The second Seal of Portsmouth, dating from the reign of Edward I, consists of two parts. On the obverse is a ship sailing a stormy sea. Two figures are in the act of rowing, two on the forecastle are blowing long horns, and two more are furling the sail. The mast is supported by strong four-cord rigging, and at the summit is a flag with four indents. Rigging also passes from the mast to the bow and stern of the vessel. The inscription runs thus: "Sigillum Commune de Portsmuthe." The reverse shows a shrine. In the centre is the Virgin Mary, on the right is St Nicholas and on the left St Thomas. And this is the appeal: "This Port O Virgin assist. O St. Nicholas cherish. O Thomas pray for."

Portsmouth's Fair Sister

1304

Gosport, which has long been regarded as the "Fair Sister of Portsmouth," owes its noble name to the fact that Henry de Blois, Bishop of Winchester, found safety there when he was cast ashore during a great storm. He named it God's Port and obtained for it a valuable charter. St Swithun is the Patron Saint.

How Portsmouth was Avenged

1385

On several occasions during the 14th Century, the French came in force and burnt the town, but this year the inhabitants were gloriously avenged. "In 1385," writes Campbell in his *Naval History*, "the French fitted out several squadrons to infest the English coasts, in which they were but too successful, yet the inhabitants of Portsmouth, to show that the martial spirit of the nation was not quite exhausted, fitted out a squadron at their own expense, which, engaging the French with equal force, took every ship and slew all but nine persons on board them, performing other gallant exploits before they returned to port.

"Hired by none, bought by none, but spurred on by their own valour and innate courage, these gallant mariners proceeded to the Seine with a small force, where they captured four and sank the same number of French vessels. Among the prizes was a barge worth 20,000 florins, which is described as having no equal for size and beauty either in England or France."

Two Round Towers are Built

1417

To render Portsmouth a securer haven, a Round Tower was commenced this year, but it was a long time before it was completed.

This briefest of Gates' entries is elaborated on later in the book, but deserves amplification. The Round Tower was originally built in wood, with a sister tower on the Gosport shore. It was rebuilt in stone about 60 years later and remained a key part of the city's defences for centuries. It was bought by the City Council in 1958.

A Bishop is Murdered

1449

The murder on January 9th, 1449, of the Bishop of Chichester near the Domus Dei, by seamen, for failing to pay the wages due to them, is thus quaintly described by the English Chronicle: "This year the Friday the IX day of Januarye, maister Adam Moleyns, bisshope of Chichestre and keper of the Kynge's prive seal, whom the Kynge sente to Portesmouth, forto make paiement of money to certayne soudiers and shipmenne for their wages, and so it happid that with boistes langage and also for abriggying of their wages, he fil in variaunce with theym and they fil on him and cruelli there kilde him."

For this crime, the town was placed under the Greater Excommunication, and as matters went very ill with the inhabitants in the years that followed, they attributed their misfortunes to this cause. It was lifted in 1508, part of the penalty being the erection of a Chapel of Expiation on the spot where the crime was committed.

The First Dry Dock in England

1496

In June, 1495, the King gave orders for the construction of a dry dock at Portsmouth, the first known to have been built in this country. Down to 1563, Portsmouth, in virtue of its dock, remained the predominant naval port. The Sovereign was the first ship to enter it on May 25th, 1496. The docking process was a serious business, as 140 men in addition to the Mariners were employed by "a day and a night." When she came out of dock on January 21st, 20 men were at work for 29 days at every tide both day and night "weying up of the piles and shorys and digging of ye clay and other rubbish between the gates."

The design of this early dry dock seems to have been crude but reasonably effective. Some form of horse-powered engine was used to draw water out of the space between the inner and outer gates, and this area was then filled with clay, stones, and rubbish to make it as watertight as possible while repair work went on.

The Square Tower is Built

1494

This year, by order from King Henry VII, the Square Tower at the end of the High Street was built and also the adjacent Platform. It was probably not designed for defensive purposes, as the Round Tower at the entrance to the Harbour was quite capable of dealing with any enemy ships seeking entrance. After the dissolution of the monasteries in 1540 it was used as a magazine, and it was due to Colonel Goring's threat to fire the powder therein that he obtained generous terms of surrender for himself and his followers when the Forces of Parliament besieged the town in 1642.

For a century or more the Tower was used as a magazine; then in 1779, under the advice of Jonas Hanway, it was transferred to the Victualling Board and converted into a store. To facilitate the shipment of provisions, a stage or small pier was built out from the Tower and this was known as the Beef Stage.

Of the remarkable Colonel Goring, and the equally remarkable Jonas Hanway, more later.

The Pride of Portsmouth

1509

This year is one of the most notable in the history of Portsmouth. The first warship known to have been built here was the Peter Pomegranate of 600 tons. Another and more notable warship, the Mary Rose, after long and careful building, was also set afloat from the Dockyard — the "wonder and admiration of all beholders." She carried 79 guns and, with the Sovereign, was the most powerfully armed that had yet existed in the British Navy. Her complement was 400 and, in a letter to the King, Sir Edward Howard described her as "Your wonder ship, the flower, I trow, of all ships that ever sailed." In 1545 a French fleet arrived at St Helens and in an engagement that ensued, the Mary Rose sank, mainly because the lower deck ports had been left open. In 1840, several guns were recovered from the wreck, one of the most curious being of wrought iron, secured by 33 loops fixed on a solid piece of elm 9 feet 6 inches long.

Pageantry at Spithead

1512

Under date of August 2nd it is recorded: "The King, desiring to see his Navie together rode to Portsmouth and there he appointed Capitaynes to the Regent and the Sovereign and with them 60 of the tallest men of the King's Guard. He made a great banquet to all the Capitaynes and everyone sware to another to defend, ayde and comfort one another without failying and this they promised before the King which committed them to God and so with great noise of minstrelsie they took their shippes which were XXV in number and of great burthen and well furnished in all things."

The same writer tells us that the sailors were dressed in white gaberdines with a Tudor rose on breast and back. The spectacle of all the ships with their flags flying from mast-head and yard-arm must have been radiant, but in the subsequent fight with the French the Regent (shown left) was blown up with her opponent. She had just been refitted at Portsmouth. The recorder adds: "The King thereupon caused a great ship to be made, such another as was never seen before in England and to be named Henri Grace a Dieu."

A Mighty Chain of Iron

1522

This year the making of a great chain was ordered, the object being to keep enemy ships from entering the harbour by stretching a "mighty chain" from Point to Blockhouse at Gosport. It was raised by capstans and supported by lighters. This was the "Mightie Chaine of yron" seen by Leland when he visited the town in 1540. In 1664, another chain was made by Edward Silvester of Gosport and he was paid £200 for the work. Dr. Quarrier, who served in the Royal William, a receiving ship at Portsmouth, in 1799–1801, wrote a letter to the press some years later stating that the last time the chain was raised was in 1801 when there were fears of a French invasion. There seems to be no record of the chain ever being used successfully. To set the matter beyond dispute whether it was in any way possible to break through a strong barrier, naval authorities allowed an experiment to be tried at the beginning of this century, with the result that a torpedo boat driven at full speed jumped the boom with perfect ease without serious damage to herself. In 1930, when some men were digging near the Round Tower, they found several links of the old chain. They were three feet nine inches in length and three inches in thickness.

John Leland seems to have been a 16th Century William Cobbett, travelling widely throughout England for about ten years after 1535 and leaving a collection of valuable descriptions. Dr. Quarrier's receiving ship was a stationary ship for naval recruits.

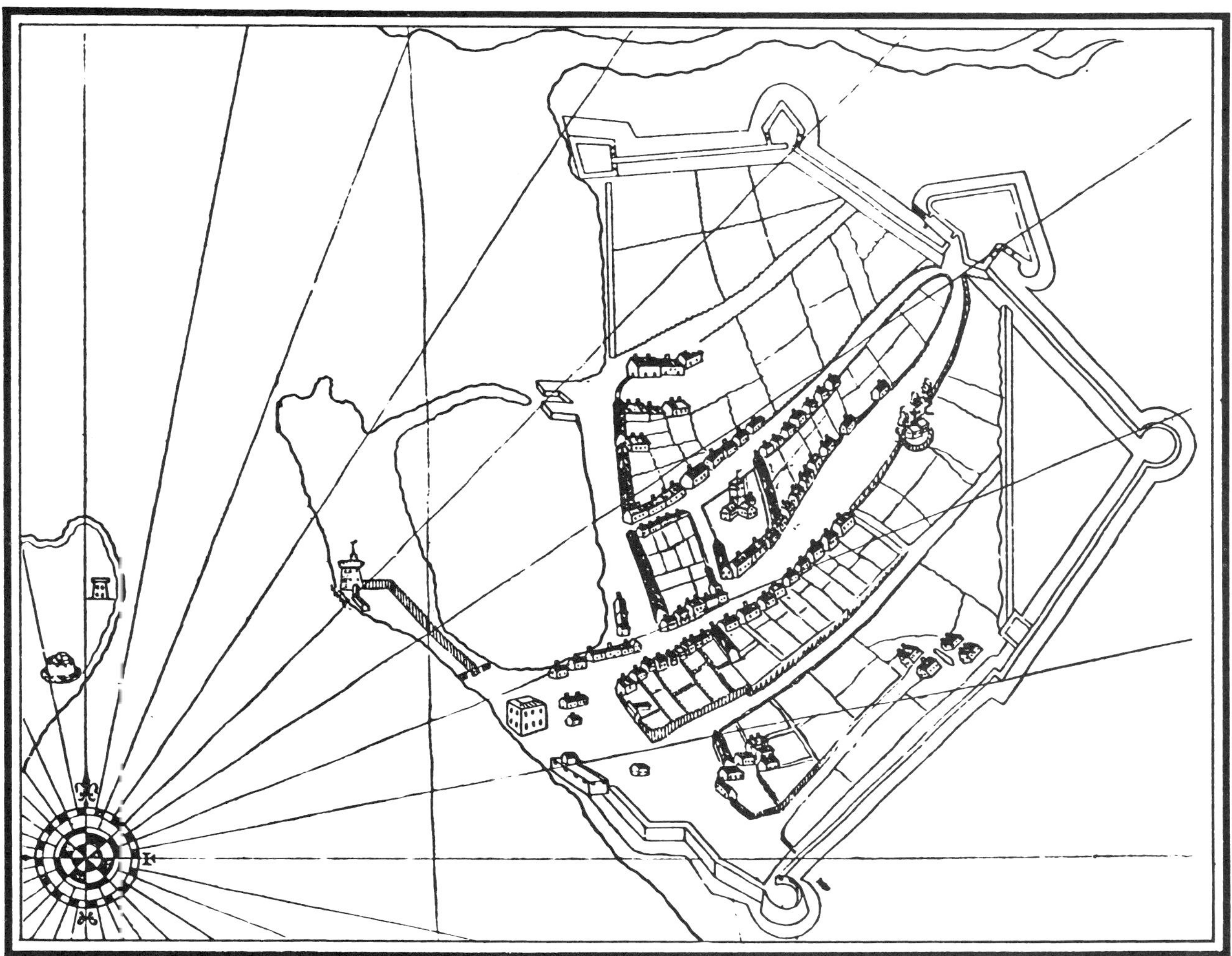

The earliest known Plan of Portsmouth

1539

This is the earliest known plan of Portsmouth. The date is not known, but it is earlier than 1540 as the "toun-house" which Leland says was built of "late tyme" does not appear upon it. On the right are the "four great brewing houses" with the spring from which they drew their water supply. Near the Domus Dei may be seen the little chapel on the Grand Parade, which the people had built as part of the penalty for the murder of a bishop who docked the wages of mariners. From the entrance to what was later known as the Mill Pond, the water is seen to extend far into the eastern portion of the town. The fortifications and the small number of houses are remarkable features.

Here is an extract from Leland's quaint description of the town when he made his tour through England: "The town of Portesmuth is murid from the est toure with a mudde waulle armid with tymbre whereon be great pieces both yron and brassen ordinauns. There is a gate of tymbre at the north est end of the toun and by it is cast up an hill of erthe diched wherein be gunnes to defend entre into the toun by land."

He was not much impressed by Gosport, which he described as a little village of fishermen.

The Castle by the South Sea

1544

The man who designed Southsea Castle was a clever and far-seeing engineer, for he placed it in such a position that for more than three centuries it formed the key to the sea defences of the port. The building was commenced in 1538, and in 1544 Antony Knyvet, the chief builder, wrote thus to the King: "It may please your Most Excellent Majesty to be so good Lord unto me to give me licence to come see your Majesty, the which shall most comfort me of all things under the Heavens and so to inform your Majesty of the state of the new fortress here, the which may be called a Castle, both for the compass, strength and beauty — and the device and fashion thereof is strange and marvellously praised of all men that have seen it, with the commodious profitable situation thereof, as well for the defence of this your Majesty's town and haven, as of the country thereabouts, the like is not within the realm. I dare say your Majesty had never so great a piece of work done and so substantial in so little time, as all skilful men that have seen it do report." It was the building of this new fortress that gave birth to a new word, "Southsea."

The building of the Castle was followed by the erection of two small circular forts on the shore, one on the present site of Lumps Fort and the other at Eastney.

Sinking of The Mary Rose

1545

This year Portsmouth witnessed an awe-inspiring spectacle. Almost the entire English Fleet, with the Great Harry as flagship of Lord Lisle, was lying at anchor at Spithead when, on July 18th, the startling news was received that a great French fleet, numbering 200 vessels large and small, was off the Isle of Wight and advancing to the anchorage. They were brought to almost within gunshot of the English ships which were anchored inside the Spit. In a perfect calm the following day, the French sent 25 galleys to the attack and the English had not a single similar vessel with which to repel it. From the one long gun which each of the galleys carried, they poured shot for an hour into the stationary hulls of the battleships and, keeping in constant motion, were themselves in perfect security. As the morning drew on, however, the offshore breeze sprang up suddenly, the large ships began to glide through the water, a number of frigates came out with "incredible swiftness," and the fortune of the day was changed. But the occasion was rendered memorable by a great misfortune. The Mary Rose had her ports open for action, the guns were run out, and in consequence of the calm had been imperfectly secured. The breeze rising suddenly, and the vessel heeling slightly over, the windward tier slipped across the deck and, as the vessel yielded farther to the weight, the lee ports were depressed below the water line. The ship instantly filled and carried down with her all on board.

Next day, the French tried to enter the harbour but failed, and then retired to the Sussex coast, whence they made their way home, disappointed and dispirited.

In describing the loss of the Mary Rose, Martin Cockram wrote: "All over, and the cry of mun, and the screech of mun. Oh Sir, up to the very heavens. And the King, he screeched right out like any maid 'Oh my Gentlemen. Oh my gallant men.' And as she lay on her beam ends Sirs, and just a-settling, the very last souls I seen was that man's father and that man's. Drowned like rattens, drowned like rattens."

Incidentally, the meeting of the fleets gave us the germ of the National Anthem, for the British watchword was "God Save King Henry" and the ringing answer came: "Long to reign over us."

Portsmouth's Loving Cup

1546

This cup is the chief gem of the collection of silver plate possessed by the Corporation. It was presented by Mrs. Bodkin, whose husband was admitted as a Burgess in 1546. It bears the motto in Latin "If God be with us, who can be against us?" Only three similar cups are known to exist, and this is the finest specimen.

Until the building of the first Town Hall, the Burgesses probably held their meetings at the King's Hall, which King Richard caused to be built when he granted the Charter of 1194. It was evidently a place of some size, as it is on record that "King John and his wife kept a roialle feast during the hole Whitsuntide theare what time they went over to treat with the King of France for peace."

A Charter for Sale

1546

It was in a strongly built Coffer, with its four locks and four separate keys, held by four Cofferers, that the Corporation kept its most precious documents, but even these precautions did not save the contents from the hands of the spoiler. The Charter of 1106 has gone, so also has the marvellous record of the Customs and Usages of the town in the 13th Century, while the Charter of 1313 was not only stolen but actually offered for sale in the streets of Portsmouth. Happily, it has been recovered but the Corporation had to pay £47 for it as the last holder had purchased it at an auction sale.

"A Great and Terryble Fire"

1557

Portsmouth suffered serious loss by the burning of the Navy Storehouses situated in what is now King Street, near the Camber. There is a manuscript at the British Museum signed by the Mayor, John Yonge, and eight other of the principal residents setting forth the losses incurred in what they describe as this "Great and Terryble ffyer," including "fyfte and three tonnes of beer with the cask." So serious was the loss that the Queen sanctioned a collection throughout the country for the distressed inhabitants.

A Watch House by the Sea

1557

To serve as a watch house, this building was erected on the Platform adjoining the Square Tower. Its final use in the years of the 19th Century was as a meeting house for naval and military officers and the favoured residents of the town. Here they read the newspapers, played cards and discussed the fate of nations.

Queen Elizabeth comes to Portsmouth

1561

This year Queen Elizabeth paid her first visit to Portsmouth, and happily resolved to use her great power and ingenuity for its development. "In our time," writes Blount, "Queen Elizabeth at great expense fortified Portsmouth so stronglie with new workes that nothing is wanting to make it a place of greate strength. Some of the Garrison mount guarde day and night at the gates. Others in the styple who, by stroke of bell, gives notice what number of horse and foot are approaching and by a flag which way they come."

"It is a remarkable fact," writes another historian, "that the expense of erecting these fortifications and others by Elizabeth were defrayed from the profits of the first State Lottery known in this Kingdom." The scheme consisted of 400,000 tickets of ten shillings each, the first prize being £5,000 made up of £3,000 in cash with £700 worth of plate and the rest in tapestries and linens. Twenty five prizes were of the value of £100 or more, and every subscriber could bask in the certainty of getting back half-a-crown.

In a later visit to Portsmouth the Queen reviewed a considerable squadron at Spithead and for the first time the yards of the ships were manned and salutes fired.

In his full History of Portsmouth, W.G. Gates points out that this lottery was obviously one of great magnitude, as the draw, according to one contemporary writer, began at the west door of St Paul's Cathedral on January 11th, 1569, and continued without a break, day and night, until May 6th that year.

Where the Women did their Washing

1562

Here is a curious and illuminating extract from the Corporation Records. "Whereas many indiscret persons not considering the Quene's affayres nor ther owne helthes, nor ye comodity of the hole towne, hath used and yet do use to wash both bucks (foul clothing) and upr clothes in the diche and springs of the four houses, we geve in charge yt none hereafter presume to do the lyke in paine of X/s for every offence."

These springs were the chief water supply of the inhabitants at this time. They were situated at the upper end of what is now Penny and St Nicholas Streets. The Four Houses referred to were the breweries which had been built there many years ago for the supply of beer for the Navy.

This warning, prompted by the generally insanitary conditions of the city, came too late for almost one third of the town's population. Within a few months, plague was sweeping Portsmouth, reaching its height in August and September of 1563.

"Bring out your Dead"

1563

This pitiful cry was heard in the streets of Portsmouth when the Plague came and carried off 300 of the inhabitants, no mean proportion in those days, when filth was allowed to lie in the streets, and the poor had not enough to eat. Here is an extract from the Parish Register, and it is not the only case in which a whole family perished:

July 8 — William, sonne to Thomas Ryse
July 23 — Antony, the sonne of Thomas Ryse
July 24 — Mary, the wyffe of Thomas Ryse
July 26 — Jane, the servant of Thomas Ryse
August 3 — Thomas Ryse
August 6 — Hary, the sonne of Thomas Ryse

The Joy of the Chancellor

1586

It was in July of this year that tobacco was first brought into England by Ralph Lane, the leader of an expedition sent out by Sir Walter Raleigh to colonise Virginia. As Lane and his crew walked the streets of Portsmouth smoking their pipes, the wonder of the populace must be left to the imagination. As well as tobacco, Lane is supposed to have brought potatoes into England for the first time. He was knighted for his services and two years later was appointed Captain of Southsea Castle. It was during the reign of Edward III that a ship arrived at Portsmouth from Spain laden with oranges, the first to be seen in this country. The King hastened to Portsmouth and bought up the entire quantity for the Queen, who was thus reminded of her Castilian home.

Beating the Bounds

1566

The picturesque ceremony of "Beating the Bounds" was performed periodically in Portsmouth for nearly 500 years. The first account we have of it is a copy of an ancient paper made by the Town Clerk, George Huish, in 1736. It begins as follows: "The pambulacyons (perambulations) of the bounds and liberties of Porthsmothe which hath contineawd for this iije yers (300 years) and more and nowe walkid and taken this vith of June Ano 1566 by the Mayer and inhabyntants there." After this introduction, the record proceeds in the quaint language of the time to describe the circuit of the town. It was customary at these ceremonies for the boys of the parish to accompany the party, carrying long reeds with which they literally beat the bounds. The boys were then bumped or swung round the boundary post so as to impress the boundaries upon their youthful memories.

The Green Post at Hilsea marks the original northern boundary of Portsmouth, and the commemorative pillar can still be seen today in London Road. Appropriately for a naval port, the water bounds were also beaten, and the day usually ended with a suitable celebration. In 1724, for instance, more than 320 pints of beer were drunk, as well as six gallons of claret and ten quarts of wine.

Training the First Volunteers

1587

So keen was the Earl of Sussex to place Portsmouth, of which he was Governor, in a position to repel the invader that he personally directed the drilling of the Trained Bands, and the first Volunteer Review took place at Hilsea. The name of the Earl stands first on the long list of the Freemen of Portsmouth.

Portsmouth and the Great Armada

1588

As soon as it was reported that the Spanish Fleet had sailed, every man in Portsmouth stood to his post, and the Queen ordered a number of the tallest and best picked men to march here. Final touches were given to the defences, arms and guns got ready, and all were keenly on the alert to repel the anticipated great assault. On July 19th, beacon fires in the Isle of Wight indicated the entrance to the Channel of the Great Armada, and the fiery signal was at once repeated by the cresset on the tower of St Thomas's Church. Watchers on Portsdown passed on the signal which called the men of England to their posts. How the Armada fled, pursued by the wrath of God and man, needs no narration here. We are only concerned with the story of Portsmouth, and there is no doubt that the local defenders would have acquitted themselves as bravely as their comrades on the sea.

Writing to the Council of State when the Armada was lying at Calais, Sir Walter Wynter stated that he was confirmed in his opinion that the Spanish fleet was intended to surprise Portsmouth and the Isle of Wight, but the course pursued by the Lord Admiral in preventing their design doubled his service towards them. Portsmouth was not slow to give expression to its gratitude by conferring upon Lord Howard the Freedom of the City.

Queen Elizabeth's Charter

1600

In a Charter granted by Queen Elizabeth, Portsmouth is described as "an ancient town having within itself from the time whereof the memory of man is not to the contrary, for the better rule and government of the same, one Mayor" and so on. This was the first Charter of definite incorporation. The initial letter is shown here. The Queen, who died in 1603, has been accused of meanness, but there is this to her credit, that she augmented the salaries of naval officers and raised the wages of seamen.

Cups that Cheer

1606

In consideration of his admission as a Burgess, Robert Lee "did give and bestow one Sylver standing Cupp, all Guilt, to remaine and goe from Mayor to Mayor for ever." It bears this inscription: "The kindnesses of friends shall never perish." Another cup was given by Sir Benjamin Berry, the Lieutenant Governor, and bore this inscription: "This swete berry from Benjamin did falle, then goode Sir Benjamin Berry it call."

Homecoming of Charles I

1623

To commemorate the landing of the Prince of Wales, later King Charles I, a memorial bust (paid for by himself) was placed in a niche on the northern front of the Square Tower. It bore this inscription: "King Charles the First, after his travels through all France into Spain, and having passed very many dangers both by sea and land, he arrived here the 5th day of October 1623. There was the greatest applause of joy for his safety throughout the Kingdom that was ever known or heard of." In the light of later events, it is not surprising that the words after the date have disappeared.

The bust remains in position to this day. The last sentence of the inscription was erased after the outbreak of the Civil War, by which time Charles's high-handed actions had alienated many of his subjects.

When Buckingham came to Portsmouth

1626

To prepare an expedition for the relief of Rochelle, the Duke of Buckingham took up his abode at the house in the High Street which belonged to John Mason and to which the magistrates granted a victualler's licence, the house being then named "The Spotted Dog." It was at this time that the Corporation conferred upon the Duke the Freedom of the Borough. In June, 1627, the expedition sailed and proved a disastrous failure. Of 7,833 men who had embarked at Portsmouth, only 2,989 returned, most of them being either sick or wounded. It was indeed declared that "Portsmouth was like to perish."

The Mayor, Henry Holt, had placed 150 sailors in two old houses belonging to him and, after burning up "20 tons of cask and ten in stacks," they pulled down the houses, burning all they could. Soon after there was great distress among the whole fleet for want of beer, and Holt wrote pleading for some of the £4,000 due to him and offering to repair the King's Brew-houses at his own expense if he were paid. His "crying debts" made him write "with watery eyes for no man would trust him."

One suspects a degree of "crocodile tears" in Holt's sad story, for when he died, his will showed a considerable fortune. He was Mayor three times, and three of his five sons also served on the Corporation, one of them becoming High Sheriff of Hampshire.

Coming Events cast their Shadows Before

1627

Sir John Oglander, Deputy Governor of Portsmouth, thus describes tragedy in the town a few days before the Duke of Buckingham was assassinated: "Ye Duke goinge to take coache out of Mason's house to goe to ye Coorte, some 300 maryners interupted him demaunding theyre paye. One amonge ye reste offered to pull ye Duke owt of his coache, on whych leaning foorth of his coache he layed handes on and caryed him into Mason's house to be kept as a prisoner; and then went foorth to them and appeased them, and soe went to ye Kinge at Sowthwike. After his departure ye Marinors demaunded restitution of their fellowe, and if Mason had not delivered him, they would have pulled down his howse by fforce, whereupon he delivered him; but ye 22nd of August ye Duke had him again arrested. A Councel of Warre was called and they condemned ye Marinor. As he wase carying to prison ye Marinors would agayne have rescued him; whereupon ye Duke and divers of his followers on horseback, havinge their swords drawne, rode down ye streete and drove all ye Marynors before them to ye Poynte Gate, in a most furious manner killing some to of them and woundinge divors. After they were aboorde, ye Duke, ye condemned Marynor, with ye Martiol and divers others, rode with him to ye execution, which presentlye wase p'formed on ye gibbett, betweene Portsmouth and Sowthsease Castel."

Captain John Mason had been warning for some time that the casual methods by which seamen were paid — or more frequently not paid — would lead to mutiny unless they were remedied. With this incident, Buckingham virtually signed his own death warrant.

How the Duke of Buckingham was Slain

1628

It is averred that the Duke of Buckingham was thrice warned of his approaching fate. Six months before the tragedy an officer named Towse, stationed at Windsor, declared that on three nights in succession he was awakened from sleep by a ghost whom he recognised as Sir George Villiers, the father of the Duke, who implored him to warn his son that unless he changed his attitude towards the people, he would not have long to live. The spirit, to confirm his identity, disclosed certain secrets known only to his son. When the warning was conveyed to the Duke, he admitted the accuracy of the revelations but failed to obey the warning. The sequel is thus described by Sir John Oglander: "Ye Duke was slain by one John Felton in ye howse att Portesmouth of a Captayne Mason where ye said Duke with his Dutches and sister Denbye laye. He was slayne by a stroke of a knyfe in ye left pappe (breast), ye partie affirminge that he did it to rid ye Commonwealthe of a monster and to free his country from that miserye that he saw itt wass like to fall into by his misgovernment."

Although the King was reported to have flung himself on his bed in a passion of tears when news of Buckingham's death reached him, many people throughout the country were overjoyed. After a spell in the Tower, the assassin was eventually hanged at Tyburn and his body taken to Portsmouth, where it was hung in chains on Southsea beach. The house in which the crime was committed still stands in High Street, Old Portsmouth.

No Chips — No Thatched Buildings

1635

The Admiralty issued strict injunctions that no shipwright should be suffered to carry away any "chips" and that in lieu thereof they were to receive the old allowance of one penny per day. The carrying away of "chips" had become a great scandal because of the wide interpretation given to the word.

As the Dockyard ran the risk of being destroyed by fire, orders were given that all thatched buildings in the vicinity should be covered with tiles. Orders were also given for the demolition of any obstruction within 40 feet of the walls or ramparts of the fortifications. Despite efforts to stamp out the practice, "chips" — or odd pieces of wood — continued to be regarded as a Dockyard perquisite until 1804, by which time the men were being allowed sixpence a day in lieu. Over the centuries the term had become so elastic that it included doors, window frames, chairs, stools, and any other wooden articles which might add comfort to a home. One master sailmaker not only had a bedstead made from "chips," but also a coffin for himself and his wife.

The Manor of Alverstoke

1641

In Saxon times Alverstoke belonged to the Priory of St Swithun, the Patron Saint of Gosport. In 1224 the Manor was transferred to the Bishop of Winchester in return for several important concessions. Under the Act of 1541 it was seized by the State and sold in 1642 to George Wither, a poet noted for his lyrics.

At the Restoration (in 1660) the Bishops regained their land and Alverstoke remained a possession of the See of Winchester until it was taken over by the Ecclesiastical Commissioners.

It was due to an accident that Portsmouth and Gosport are not one city. Under the Charter of Charles II, dated 1632, they were joined together for administrative purposes, much to the indignation of the Gosportonians. But by lucky chance the Charter of Charles I, which contained far better conditions, had never been officially surrendered, and after the death of Charles II it was recovered and became the governing Charter until the passing of the Municipal Corporations Act in 1835. Thus was Gosport released from its absorption, left to its own devices and the framing of its own destiny. And let it be truly said that Gosport has fully justified its separate existence.

Gates admitted that he viewed Gosport "with loving eyes," having been born in 1856 in a cottage on the border of an orchard in Spring Garden Lane.

Portsmouth declares for the King

1642

At the outbreak of the Civil War, the town was governed by the notorious Colonel Goring, who held it for the King until the forces of Parliament laid it under siege and soon brought it to subjection.

Seven warships blockaded the town and someone on board the Paragon said the greatest harmony was the thundering of cannon both by day and night. To aid the people of Portsea Island, whose sheep, cattle and corn were being seized to feed the garrison, men were landed from the squadron engaged in the blockade, and seamen ferried numerous women and children over to Hayling Island.

Portsmouth was also bombarded from Gosport, but with little effect, as the following description shows: "Friday night they shot not much from Gosport but on Sept. 3rd they played with their ordnance and shot through the tower of the church and brake one of the bells and shot against the tower again and that rebounded and fell into the church and shot down a top of a house near the end of the church." Confirmation of this statement came as recently as 1930, when two ancient cannon balls were discovered during some excavations near the church.

Goring had already changed his allegiance twice before the outbreak of war, and was reckoned as unreliable to say the least. The Earl of Clarendon took a more severe view and wrote that "on account of his private vices of drunkenness, cruelty, and rapacity, and of his political intimidity and treachery, scarely anyone was more unworthy to be entrusted with any important matters for counsel or execution."

Southsea Castle is Captured

1642

The following official account of the capture of Southsea Castle merits full reproduction here: "1642, on Saturday, September 3rd, in the night, the Parliament forces took Sousey Castle, w'ch lyes a mile from the toun upon the sea, and the way thither is on the sea sands. The captaine of the castel, his name was Challiner, who on Saturday had been at Portsmouth, and in the evening went home to the castell, and his souldiers took horseloads of provisions, biscuit, meal and other necessaries wy them. They reported he had more drinke in his head than was befitting such a tyme and service, and the tounsmen gave out that he had been bribed wy money to yield the castel up, but 'twas false, tho the first may be true, yet was not that neither any furtherence to the taking of it, for thus it was. Here were eighty musqueteers and others that came that night to the walle of the castel and under their ordnance, and had wy them a very good engineer and thirty-five scaling ladders, and the whole company in the castel were but twelve commanders or officers, who were all not able to deal wy ours in such a disadvantage; wherefore ours having suddenly and silently scaled the walls, called unto them, advised them what to do, shewing the advantage we had over them, and therefore their danger if they resisted; who seeing the same immediately yielded the castel to us, whereupon our triumph at our taking it was plainly heard about two of the clock in the morning into the towne; and as soon as they were masters of the castel they discharged two pieces of the castel ordnance against the towne, which capitulated the next day."

The account referred to is entitled "God in the Mount; or England's Parliamentary Chronicle" by J. Vicars.

Colonel Goring and his Boon Companions

1642

"The people of Newport, Isle of Wight, were scandalised by the sight of their Worshipful Governor (Gerome, Earl of Portland) with his boon companions Nicholas Weston and the dissolute Colonel Goring, Governor of Portsmouth, marching in drunken revelry towards the Town Gallows. At each health they drank they tore each others bands and raiment till, by the time they reached their destination, their clothes and shirts were in tatters. Then Goring mounted the ladder and with tipsy gravity delivered his last dying speech to the bystanders advising them to take warning by his unhappy end."

When Colonel Goring realised that all was lost, he threatened to blow up the magazine, which was located in the Square Tower, and as there was sufficient powder to destroy the whole town, the Parliamentary General allowed him and the other insurgent officers to embark on a vessel bound for Holland. Goring held on to the key of the magazine to the last and then threw it into the harbour as the ship sailed. There it remained until the close of the 19th century, when it was recovered and placed in the Public Museum.

Goring returned to England, and for a time commanded the Royal Forces in the West, but his conduct was so outrageous that he had to seek refuge on the Continent. He was last seen in the streets of Madrid, very ill, quite destitute and dressed in the habit of a Dominican Friar.

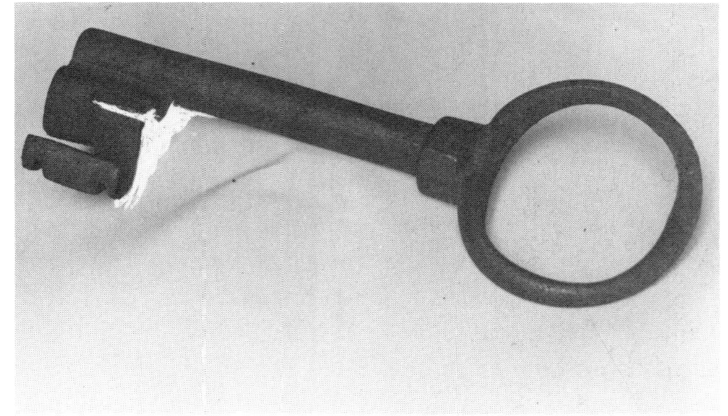

The Defence of Portsbridge

1643

In August a newspaper run by the King's Party gave the following interesting item of news from Portsmouth: "It was also signified from thence that the Lady Norton, mother of that most noble colonel who hath done such wonders of late days, and Governess for the present of the town of Portsmouth — for the Committee dare do nothing without her advice — was very busily employed in making some new works about Portsey Bridge; and was not only every day in person amongst the workmen but brought with her also every day 30 or 40 maids and women in a cart (they may live to be so coached hereafter) to dig and labour in the trenches." Thus does history repeat itself, for close to the spot where Dame Norton's maids dug trenches in 1643, hundreds of women were engaged during the Great War of 1914–1918 in preparing material for use against the common enemy.

Gosport under Siege

1645

In January, Portsmouth was threatened with another siege, this time by the forces of the King under Colonel Goring. They came near to Portsbridge, but finding the garrison strong and on the alert, they wisely retreated, some of the stragglers being killed.

Writing on January 5th, Captain (afterwards Admiral) Penn said: "Colonel Goring, his forces, came down and plundered the town of Gosport and fired some 24 houses. We, the Fellowship and Swiftsure, shot divers pieces of ordnance to them."

More attention was now given to the defences there, two forts being constructed near the shore, one known as Charles Fort being on Gosport Hard, and the other, Fort James, on Rat Island, otherwise known as Burrough Castle. Before the days of wireless telegraphy, the carrier pigeons of the Navy had their home there

Parliament Joan

1653

If the sound of the Battle off the Isle of Wight on February 19th was not heard in Portsmouth, there was soon ample evidence of the severity of the fight in the arrival of crippled ships and wounded men, including General Blake, who was lodged at the humble Colliers Arms. A memorable incident in connection with this victory is the nursing of the sick and wounded by Elisabeth Aitkin, popularly known as "Parliament Joan." She had nursed wounded soldiers during the Civil War and now came to Portsmouth, where she spent all her own money in addition to grants from the Government.

The battle referred to occurred during the First Dutch War (1652–54). Admiral Robert Blake — also known as General — was wounded in the thigh by a splinter.

The First Hampshire

1653

The first Hampshire, built at Portsmouth this year, had a distinguished career and a sad ending. She was at the attack on Porto Farina, was with Holmes when he made his "Bonfire," was Narborough's flagship when he defeated four Tripolitan men-of-war, helped in the attack on San Domingo, and then, being attacked by several armed ships, sank with her colours flying. A new dry dock was under construction at Portsmouth, and the Corporation in a burst of patriotism contributed £500 towards the cost. The event was happily marked by the capture of a rich Spanish convoy. Of eight vessels, only two escaped. The gold and silver proved of great value. It was landed here and conveyed by waggon to London, where it was triumphantly paraded through the streets.

Parson Teonge kept a Diary

1653

The Bristol, of 40 guns, launched at Portsmouth this year, did much honourable service. For a time Henry Teonge was her chaplain, and he left a most interesting diary of his naval services. Here are extracts:

> June 16th, 1678: The scolding woman was well washt.
>
> August 16th: A seaman had 20 lashes with a cat-o'-nine-tails and was then washt with salt water for stealing our carpenter's mate's wife's ring.
>
> September 8th: This day I preacht a sermon at Caesar's Church, there being the Mayor of Portsmouth and several other gentlemen present. We dined at the inn there and were very merry.

The Ropemakers of Portsmouth

1653

Ropemaking was a popular industry in Portsmouth long before a ropewalk was constructed in the Dockyard. Where Kent Street is now there was an important ropewalk, and the sketch shows the class of houses the ropemakers inhabited. Another ropewalk was in front of what is now Landport Terrace, and a third branched off Church Street, Landport. It became a custom whenever royalty came to Portsmouth for the ropemakers to precede the carriage. They carried white staves, wore blue sashes across the shoulder, and carried banners.

A Famous Freeman

1653

George Monk, the Duke of Albemarle, was admitted to the Freedom of Portsmouth in recognition of his great naval services. In May of this year he commanded the fleet in conjunction with General Deane, and on the death of the latter in the heat of battle, he cast his cloak over the mangled body lest the crew might be discouraged by the sight. He also commanded the fleet in the action in which the famous Dutch Admiral Van Tromp was killed. Later he helped to bring about the restoration of the King.

A Link with Pennsylvania

1654

Admiral Sir William Penn, father of William Penn, the founder of Pennsylvania, was this year admitted to the Freedom of Portsmouth. He had distinguished himself on many occasions, but because he failed in an expedition to the West Indies, he was committed to the Tower by Cromwell. At the Restoration, he was released, knighted, and appointed a Commissioner at the Admiralty. He was present at the capture of Jamaica and was Great Captain Commander under the Duke of York when a decisive victory was gained over the Dutch.

The Ancient Hospital of St Nicholas

1658

The former residential portion of the Domus Dei, which had been used as an armoury since the Dissolution of the Monasteries in 1540, was this year converted into a residence for the Governor, and as such it continued for 300 years. Many famous people were entertained there, and it was in the great hall of the building that the wedding of Catherine of Braganza and King Charles II was celebrated. Its last official use was when the Allied Sovereigns were entertained there in 1814.

The Story of the Great Mace

1658

Josiah Childe, a merchant largely engaged in the manufacture of biscuits for the Navy, became Mayor of the Borough and, at the same time, his brother John represented the Borough in Parliament. In 1662, both were ejected from the Corporation for suspected disloyalty and Portsmouth knew them no more, except as the donors of the handsome silver mace which is still carried as the chief emblem of authority. The two small maces were used as the insignia of the Water Bailiffs.

The Childes were among nearly 100 leading Portsmouth figures who fell victim to a purge by the newly-restored King Charles II. Josiah went back to London, was knighted in 1678, became Governor of the East India Company, and died worth a fortune.

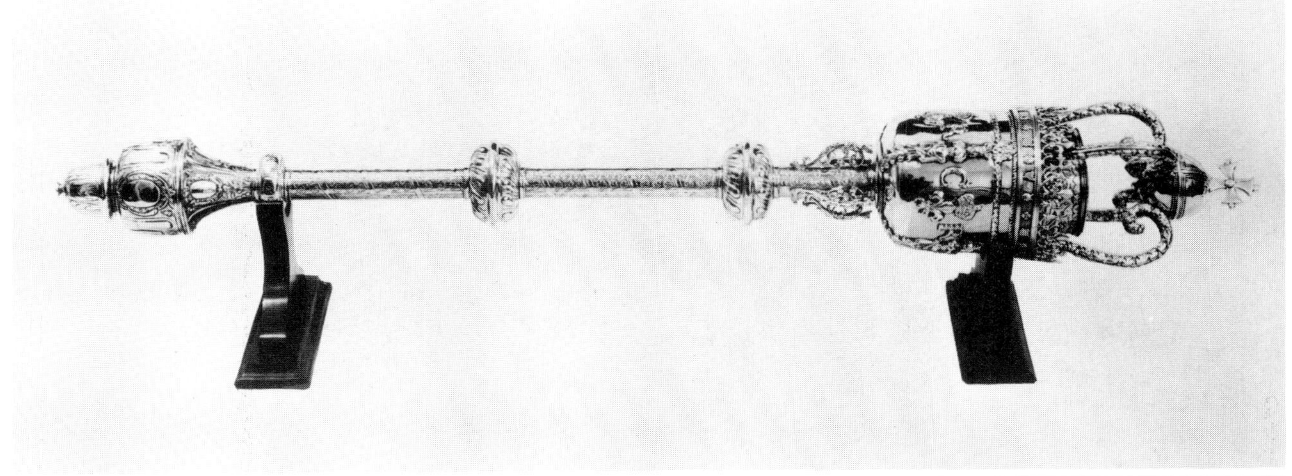

Samuel Pepys paid the Reckoning

1662

Among the many remarkable men who have been honoured with the Freedom of Portsmouth, a foremost place must be given to Samuel Pepys, the diarist beyond compare. Here is what he wrote under date April 30th, 1662: "During the afternoon comes Mr. Stevenson to tell me that the Mayor and Burgesses desire my acceptance of a Burgess-ship and were ready at the Mayor's to make me one. So I went and there they all were ready, and did with much civility give me my oath and, by custom, shake me all by the hand. So I took them to a tavern and made them drink, and paying the reckoning went away. It cost me a piece of gold to the Town Clerk and ten shillings to the Bayliffes, and spent five shillings."

The following extract from his famous diary shows how Pepys enjoyed himself at Portsmouth. "After our work was done, Sir G. Carteret, Sir William Pen and I walked forth and I spied Mrs. Pierce and another lady passing by. So I went to the ladies and walked them up and down, and gave them wine and sweetmeat, and were very merry. And then came the Doctor and we took them by coach to their lodging, which was very poor but the best they could get, and such as made much mirth among us. So I appointed one to watch when the Gates of the Town were ready to be shut and to give us notice. And so the Doctor and I staid with them playing and laughing, but at last were forced to bid them good-night for fear of being locked into the Town all night. So we walked to the Yard designing to prevent our going to London to-morrow, that we might be merry with these ladies which I did. So to supper and merrily to bed."

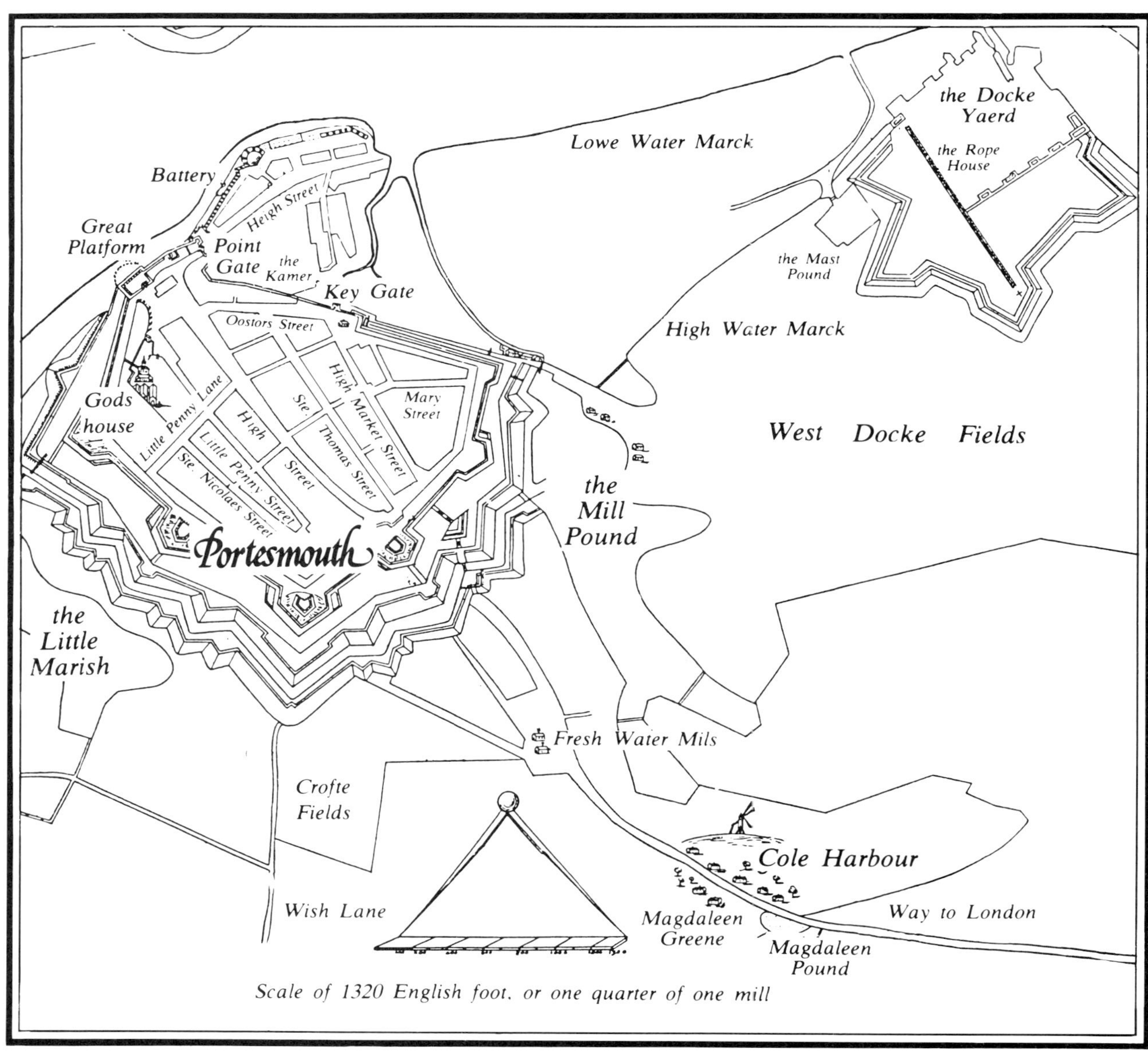

Portsmouth Re-Fortified

1662

A famous Dutch engineer named Sir Bernard de Gomme was entrusted with the task of re-planning the fortifications. The plan here reproduced is of peculiar interest as it shows the general layout of the town. Portsea had not yet been born upon the West Docke Fields, but the four buildings shown on the banks of the Mill Pond include at least one which had stood there for centuries.

A Royal Bride from Portugal

1662

On May 14th, Catherine of Braganza, the Portuguese bride chosen for King Charles II, landed at Portsmouth. The Corporation were there in their gowns with a present and speech ready to entertain her, while the guns of the fleet and fortress "echoed to one another the loud proclamation of their joy."

The diarist John Evelyn wrote: "The Queen arrived with a train of Portuguese ladies in their monstrous fardingales or guard-infantas (an early form of crinoline); their complexions olivador and sufficiently disagreeable; Her Majesty in the same habit, her foretop long and turned aside very strangely. She was yet of the handsomest countenance of all the rest and, though low of stature, prettily shaped, languishing and excellent eyes; her teeth wronging her mouth by sticking a little too far out; for the rest, lovely enough."

The King did not arrive to greet his bride until May 20th, and in a letter to Lord Clarendon, he wrote: "Her face is not so exact to be called a beauty, though her eyes are excellent good. She has much agreeableness, and I think she must be as good a woman as ever was born." The marriage took place two days later in the Guest Chamber of Government House, and the certificate is still preserved at Portsmouth Cathedral.

When the King Reviewed his Fleet

1662

In May, Charles II reviewed his fleet at Spithead, and here is a description of the ceremony observed. "The ship is in every part to be made neat and predie and to be trimmed with all her flags. On the first keen of the Royal Barge, the ship's decks, tops and yards are to be manned and as it were hung with men. Upon the nearer approach of the Royal Barge the trumpets are to sound until he come within less than musket of the ship's side. Then all such as carry whistles are to whistle his welcome three several times and in every interim the ship's whole company are to hail him with a joynt shout after the custom of the sea."

We are further told that the ship's side and the ladder were to be manned with "the primest and best fashioned men," and the Captain is to be ready to receive the King upon his knee. His Majesty was to be entertained with music, and as he went over the ship's side when he departed, the trumpets were to sound "A loath to depart."

During his visit the King inspected the work on the Royal Charles, with which he was "infinitely pleased." She was the largest vessel in England at that time.

In this connection it is interesting to note that Grinling Gibbons, the famous carver, started his career in Portsmouth Dockyard, where he was engaged as a boy on the work of carving figureheads for warships. While still in his struggling days he made his way to London, where his work was brought to the notice of Charles II, who gave him commissions which led to fame and fortune.

Sorrows of a Dockyard Commissioner

1665

Writing to the Admiralty, Commissioner Thomas Middleton said: "To tell you of the strayght I have been put to sence my cominge to Portsmouth for my accomodation would be to small purpose, and but that I have a boddy that can indure any thinge I hadd been dead. Wheare I now am, wee are forsceed to packe nyne people to sleepe in a roome not above 16 foot one way by 12 the other. Wee are 26 in famyly in Mr. Mayoures house, nyne of which are small children. What comfort can a man have in such a condition soe being together?" In another letter the Commissioner wrote praying for money to "stop the bawlings and impatience of these people, especially of their wives whose tongues are as foul as the daughters of Billingsgate." The Commissioner, however, was not without sympathy, as he lent the men ten shillings apiece from his own purse.

Colonel Middleton's gesture was less magnanimous than Gates would have it appear. The money was paid to prevent a mutiny among soldiers, seamen, and workmen who found it difficult to get the wages due to them. His plea for better accommodation led Pepys, then Secretary to the Admiralty, to authorise him to build a house in the dockyard.

A Famous and Favourite Freeman

1671

Edward, Earl of Sandwich, who was this year added to the Freemen of Portsmouth, was a favourite of the people, and one of the streets in the new building was named after him. On the outbreak of the Civil War he joined the Parliamentary Forces. Later he was made General-at-Sea and served with Blake. At the end of the Cromwell régime he reverted to the Royalists, won the Fleet over to his side, and brought Charles back to England. Again appointed General-at-Sea, he distinguished himself at the Battle of Lowestoft, and perished in the fight at Southwold Bay.

Many Ran Away from the First Naval Hospital

1672

In his History of Haslar Hospital, Fleet Surgeon William Tate thus refers to the early plan of treating naval patients in private hospitals at so much per head. In the diary of Dr. Yonge, of Plymouth, is an account "amusing in its candour." When war broke out with the Dutch in 1672, he obtained a surgeon's place in such a hospital set up for the sick and wounded. He writes: "My pay was five shillings per diem constant and three pence for each man for medicine. I had also half-a-crown a day for each mate and a mate for every 30 men, so that I had sometimes four mates pay but one mate in being. The three pence per man seemed worst, but considering that many ran away as soon as they came, that most others were scurvy which costs little, the three pence per man did well enough, though it was a small reward."

The Captain of the Mary Rose

1675

Sir John Kempthorne, captain of the Mary Rose, first acquired fame by defeating seven Algerian pirates. In 1675, he was appointed Naval Commissioner at Portsmouth and when he died, his body was buried in the ancient Church of St Thomas, now a cathedral. A tablet to his memory is thus inscribed:

"Here beneath this stone doth lye
As much valour as could dye
Who in his life did vigour give
To as much justice as could live,
But death which ne'er could him dismay
Unkindly snatch'd him hence away."

In 1923, a model of the Mary Rose was presented to the Portsmouth Cathedral by Mr. Clemence Langford, a native of Portsea, and hoisted with full naval honours in which many admirals took part.

The Scaffold ends All

1676

In August of this year John Hickes conducted the first Nonconformist Baptism in Portsmouth, the ceremony being performed in what came appropriately to be known at Eastney as "The Glory Hole." The following year Hickes was fined £20 for "preaching and teaching in a Sedicious Conventicle, known as the Golden Ball," which was at the corner of Barrack and Penny Streets.

Hickes fought on the side of the Duke of Monmouth at Sedgmoor and after escaping from the battlefield, he was given shelter by Lady Lisle in her house at Ringwood. For this she was tried by Judge Jeffreys and condemned to be burnt alive, but the King commuted this savage sentence to beheading. Hickes was hanged.

Judge Jeffreys, "of infamous memory," was Recorder of Portsmouth and one of its Freemen. In 1682 he died miserably in the Tower of London, "having dwindled from a corpulent man to a skeleton."

Hickes took no part in the actual fighting during Monmouth's rebellion against James I, although he admitted trying to persuade Royalist prisoners to join the insurgents. He was hanged at Glastonbury in October, 1685. Lady Lisle was particularly unfortunate. At her trial in Winchester, the jury three times brought in a "Not guilty" verdict, but the notorious Jeffreys threatened and bullied them until they reversed it.

The First Military Barracks

1680

This year a hospital for sick and wounded soldiers was built on the site of an ancient priory, known as St Mary of Closse, at the western end of St Mary Street. In 1694 it was converted into ordinary barracks, the first of its kind in the kingdom. During alterations early in the 20th Century, workmen uncovered an arch which had evidently formed part of the priory which gave the name of St Mary to one of the most ancient thoroughfares in old Portsmouth. And a few years ago, some of the iconoclasts in the Town Council caused this name to be blotted out in favour of the meaningless Highbury Street.

"Loyalty Everywhere"

1683

When King Charles II conferred upon Louise de Querouaille, one of his mistresses, the title of Duchess of Portsmouth, she presented to the Corporation a pair of massive silver flagons bearing the strange motto "Loyalty Everywhere."

Touching for the King's Evil

1685

In the Portsmouth Parish Register there is a form of certificate granted to afflicted persons in order to entitle them to the Royal Touch: "We, the Minister and Churchwarden of the Town and Parish of Portsmouth, do hereby certify that 'A B' of the parish is afflicted as we are creditably informed with the disease commonly called the King's Evil and, to the best of our knowledge, has not heretofore been touched by His Majesty for the said disease." King Charles II performed the ceremony on one occasion when he came to the town, and James II touched 151 people, the last occasion being in 1685. The ceremony was performed upon the open space now known as Governor's Green. In the presence of the Court Chaplain, who offered certain prayers, the King touched each sufferer, who was then presented with a metal "Touchpiece" pierced so that it might be suspended by a ribbon round the neck. There is no local record of the effect, if any, of this "Touching."

The disease thus referred to was scrofula, an early form of tuberculosis which it was believed could be cured by the royal touch.

Two Famous Freemen

1685

Portsmouth made a distinguished addition to its list of Freemen when it conferred the honour upon The Right Reverend Thomas Ken, one of the seven Bishops sent to the Tower for refusing the king's command. Even more worthy of remembrance is he as the author of two of the most beautiful of English hymns, "Awake my soul and with the Sun," and "Glory to Thee my God this night."

Another Freeman of Portsmouth was Jonathan Trelawney, Bishop of Winchester, another of the seven Bishops sent prisoner to the Tower for disputing the legality of the "Declaration of Indulgences."

The Youngest Governor of Portsmouth

1687

King James II gave a surprise collection of silver plate to the Church of St Thomas. Three weeks later, his natural son, James Fitzjames, was appointed Governor of Portsmouth. Was the gift of plate intended to soothe any irritation that might arise in the town by the King appointing his 19-year-old natural son to such an important position?

This was all part of James II's plan to place his Catholic supporters in key positions. At the same time, he filled the Portsmouth garrison — of which his son was Colonel-in-Chief — with Irish Catholic soldiers. When the regiment's senior officers protested, they were court-martialled and cashiered.

King James's Gate

1687

The first of the historic gates of Portsmouth was that of King James II, which separated the old town from the district known as Point. It was an imposing structure in the Venetian style, with double columns on each side of the archway, an entablature supporting a circular tower and ball, with ornamental spires on each side. An inscription ran "Jacobus Secundus A.R. III An Dom 1687." A heavy drawbridge was in front, crossing an inlet from the sea into the Camber. An emasculated portion of this beautiful gate now stands at the entrance to the Officers' Recreation Ground.

This elegant structure spanned what is now Broad Street, just beyond the Sally Port. It was taken down in the 1870s and re-erected in the Royal Naval Barracks, then moved once more to its present site in Burnaby Road at the entrance to the United Services' ground.

A Famous Admiral and Freeman

1698

This year Admiral Sir George Rooke was chosen as one of the Members of Parliament for Portsmouth and at the same time made one of its Freemen. Not only was he a most successful sea captain but a worthy and generous man. With a portion of his prize money he paid for apprenticeship fees of many poor orphans of Portsmouth, and he it was who helped to secure a set of bells for St Thomas's Church. He is reported to have made the following pathetic answer to those who were present at the execution of his will, and who expressed surprise at the smallness of his fortune: "I do not leave much but what I leave was honestly gotten, it never cost a sailor a tear nor the nation a farthing."

Portsmouth honours Peter the Great

1698

In March, Peter the Great visited Portsmouth and the first naval sham fight was arranged in his honour. It is thus described by the "Flying Post," a newspaper of the period:

"The representation of a sea engagement was excellently performed and continued a considerable time, each ship having twelve pounds of powder allowed, but all the bullets were locked up in the hold for fear the sailors might mistake."

Another account states that there were two sham fights, so each ship took her opposite and fired three broadsides.

A Governor Pious and Pitiless

1701

Sir John Gibson, Lieutenant-Governor of Portsmouth at this time, was a strange mixture of piety and ferocity. He it was who ordered the cruel punishment of the "Wooden Horse" for many poor soldiers, or confined them in a deep dungeon near the Quay Gate. It was the same man who regularly attended the services at St Thomas's Church and provided a pair of handsome gates in Church Lane. This lane, which is shown in the earliest plans of Portsmouth, has now been absorbed by the Cathedral.

Gibson, who was Lieutenant-Governor from 1689 until his death in 1717, became one of Portsmouth's two M.P.s in 1701 and was knighted four years later. The dungeon referred to was known as "Johnny Gibson's Hole," and stories of the time recounted how soldiers were incarcerated there for trifling misdemeanours until they almost starved to death. The "Wooden Horse" was a device on which defaulters were set astride, with two or more muskets strapped to each foot, in front of the door of Gibson's house in Grand Parade.

Portsea is Born

1703

Being on a visit to Portsmouth, Queen Anne granted the request of the Dockyard shipwrights to build for themselves houses on what was then known as Portsmouth Common. They had been threatened by Governor Gibson that he would turn the guns of the garrison upon them if they dared to lay one brick on another. Queen Street and Prince George Street commemorate this mark of Royal favour. The Prince was also granted the Freedom of the Borough.

The rapid growth of the town "without the walls" was, however, viewed with disfavour by those living within the old boundaries, and in October, 1717, the Leet Jury made the following Presentment:

"We present that the place called The Hard, lately made in the waterside nigh the Dock Gate, within the Liberties of this Borough, is a very great damage to the inhabitants of this Borough and tends to the impoverishing of the same."

Notwithstanding this, the child soon surpassed the mother in size, if not in importance, and at the first census taken in 1801, the population of Portsea was 24,327, while that of Portsmouth was 7,839.

In the early days of Portsea, a mock ceremony would take place every May Day to elect a Mayor and Corporation. The occasion was apparently marked by "much buffoonery and licentiousness."

The Bells of St Thomas

1703

Thanks to Prince George of Denmark and Admiral Sir George Rooke, a set of eight bells was provided for St Thomas's Church tower and a clock was given by the Mayor, William Brandon. A sequel told by the historian W.H. Saunders relates: "Well knowing that the bells unless they are sounded are of no use, and that bell ringers, tho' a very noisy, are often a very idle set of personages who won't ring unless they are paid, or have a leg of mutton and turnips provided for supper by mine host of the Eight Bells, with flagons of Sir Thomas Ridge's stout ales — he, at his own proper cost by curious machinery attached to a large clock to set St Thomas's bells chiming every four hours in spite of the ringers who had risen in open rebellion on December 21st at noon, the ears of the listening town's people were astonished and their pious feelings excited by the euphonious bells resounding in long metre the Old Hundredth Psalm and the hymn of the Sicilian Mariners."

A "Golden Barque" was also placed in position on the tower of St Thomas's to serve as a weather vane and whenever it was taken down, young children were placed within it in the belief that it would ensure their safety at sea.

Ridge's Brewhouses, owned by a celebrated family of brewers and councillors, stood on the west side of High Street, Old Portsmouth, where the Town Hall was later built.

The Newcastle sinks at Spithead

1703

On November 26th the country was swept by the greatest storm on record. In the region traversed by it, forests of trees were uprooted, 13 men-of-war were wrecked, 800 houses and 400 windmills blown down, and Eddystone Lighthouse destroyed. The Newcastle was overwhelmed at Spithead and 200 of her crew perished.

The Newcastle was one of 13 ships wrecked around the coasts of Great Britain, most of them with heavy loss of life. One contemporary account said that "Portsmouth, Plymouth, Weymouth and most of our seaport towns looked as if they had been bombarded, and the damage of them is not easily computed."

A Dockyard Church

1704

The Church of St Anne was built by the voluntary contributions of the officers and men of the Navy and Dockyard and also endowed by them. In 1785 it became necessary to take down the building and the Admiralty provided another at public expense. It was damaged, but not destroyed, when the Germans attacked the town in 1941. In the cupola hangs the bell of the Royal George. In 1882 the convicts then employed in Portsmouth made a noble contribution of a polished granite font carved entirely by themselves.

Bear Baiting and Cock Fighting

1704

The amusements of the dwellers in old Portsmouth were not of an elevating character. Gambling, ratting and bull-baiting appear to have been the principal recreations. In October, 1704, the Grand Jury made Presentment "that the anointing of Ratts with Turpentine and putting fire to them is of dangerous consequence, especially in this Towne where there are Magazeens of Powder, and tends to the setting of the dwelling houses of the Inhabitants on fire." It was also the custom to indulge in a little bull-baiting in Broad Street on Shrove Tuesday, and cock fighting was so general that the magistrates issued a notice prohibiting it because of the "riotts, quarells and other mischiefs" occasioned thereby.

The Great Salterns

1705

The land on the eastern side of the island of Portsea, known as the Great Salterns, was reclaimed from the harbour about this time. It was so named because of the existence nearby of a Little Salterns, the evaporation of sea water for the salt it contained having been a very ancient industry.

Great Salterns was incorporated into the old county borough in 1895 and eventually converted into a golf course and playing fields.

500 Hands Lost in Melancholy Catastrophe

1711

On October 15th, 1711, the Edgar, a 70-gun ship, was lying at Spithead when from some cause never discovered, she blew up with dreadful results. Over 500 lives were lost by this melancholy catastrophe, which was regarded as very ominous by the men of the fleet because she was the oldest vessel in the Navy. Some, indeed, went so far as to affirm that she was actually the ship in which King Edgar sailed, some part of the old vessel being constantly preserved every time she had been rebuilt.

"The Friend and Father of the Poor"

1712

Jonas Hanway, born this year at a house in St George's Square, devoted his life to deeds of service for the poor and distressed. Having spent a large fortune in deeds of philanthropy, he was appointed a Commissioner for victualling the Navy. His headquarters were over the Square Tower at the end of the High Street, and he converted an old landing stage into a pier from which he was able to serve the fleet at Spithead.

Hanway will always be famous for his umbrella. He was the first man to carry one in the streets of London. Otherwise, they were said to be used only by seamstresses carrying home their work and by parsons at funerals. The Hanway sample would have caught the eye under any circumstances. It was of Persian manufacture, light green outside and pale pink within. Its handle was carved and had a joint in the middle so that he could fold it up and place it in his coat pocket.

From the umbrella's exotic description, it is small wonder that Jonas Hanway carried it around fashionable London for 30 years before anyone saw fit to follow his example. He died in 1786, and a memorial to him can be found in Westminster Abbey.

"Is Queen Anne Dead?"

1714

This question might be heard when the people of Portsmouth met in joyous mood. John Carter, member of a leading family, was in London when the Queen died and, hastening home, was the first to announce the news. Governor Gibson, who was a bit of a terror, declared it to be a false and even seditious report and threatened Carter with condign punishment if he repeated it. But the tables were turned when the news was confirmed, and it became a standing joke to ask your friend when Gibson was near: "Is Queen Anne dead?"

Lively Baptisms at Eastney

1716

This year the first Nonconformist Chapel was built in the High Street and it preserved its original appearance until the Germans ruined it in 1941. The leader of the Baptists before the chapel was erected was James Osmond, who kept a small farm at Eastney. Meetings were held there and converts baptised in a pond which was well stocked with carp, frogs, and sticklebacks.

Cat-of-nine-tails for a Woman

1722

Here is sentence of whipping on a woman convicted of stealing a Holland apron worth ninepence:

> "Between the hours of eleven and twelve in the forenoon she is to be brought to the publick Whipping Post in the Market Place (this was in the High Street, behind the Town Hall) and to be stript from the middle upwards and then fixed to the said Whipping Post and there receive Twenty lashes with a Cat-of-Nine-Tails from the hands of the Comon Beadle on her naked back and till the same shall be bloody and then return to the said Gaol and there remain until her fees be paid."

The First Poorhouse

1725

The first Poorhouse in Portsmouth was built this year by public subscription, at the northern end of Warblington Street. The inmates appear to have been well treated, many quarts of brandy being drunk and many pounds of tobacco smoked in the course of a year. Some time later a Poorhouse for Portsea was built at the corner of Elm Road, Mile End.

"A Common Nuisance of Ill Consequence"

1726

Here is a copy of a Presentment made by the Grand Jury at the Quarter Sessions:

"That the great number of alehouses, victualling houses, punch houses and other tippling houses in the back streets and by-places of this Towne and the Libertys thereof (and the daily increase thereof) tends to the impoverishment of some and gives too great a liberty of Intemperance to others, the Inhabitants of the said Towne, and is a common Nuisance of ill consequince."

The Royal Naval Academy

1729

This year the Royal Naval Academy at Portsmouth was established and continued to be a training ground for cadets and officers until 1872, when it transferred to Greenwich. In a description of Portsmouth this year, Stephen Martin Leake, then employed in the Navy Pay Office, thus refers to the Dockyard: "It is a fine place, more compact than any other, and the docks are stone, which in others are wood. The Yard is enclosed by a high wall. They have a Chapel for the use of the Yard and, I do assure you, a good Dock Regiment."

Home of the Early Club

1729

One of the strangest of clubs was in favour in Portsmouth at this time. Its home was the ancient hotel at the corner of Grand Parade. Here is the description of it written by Martin Leake:

"We have clubs enough in London, never parting until early in the morning, but this does not meet till that time, and the members consist of the most sensible men in the place. Their hour is four in the morning, where they meet without disturbing the coffee people or their own families. The fire is laid in the Coffee Room and everything ready that they may want, overnight. He that comes first lets himself in, strikes a light, lights the fire and puts on the kettle. When so many are met, the coffee is made and after spending an hour drinking coffee, reading the news and talking politics, they separate."

This home of the Early Club was formerly the meeting house of captains of the Navy. In the olden time, before lieutenants wore epaulettes and captains wore red breeches, three-cornered hats, buckles and pigtails, it was not uncommon to see captains of the Royal Navy sitting outside this house on forms smoking long pipes.

The hotel referred to was Piles' Coffee House. It obviously enjoyed considerable popularity, but not with Leake, who observed that it was "neither pleasant nor wholesome to go abroad till the sun has blessed the earth and exhaled the vapours of the night."

King George's Gate

1734

The gate, erected this year and known as the Quay or King George's Gate, gave access to the Camber. It was a noble structure in the rustic style, adorned with massive pillars and entablature of fine proportions. Prior to its erection, entrance from the town at this point was through a small arch in the encircling wall.

This gate, in the area between what is now Gunwharf Road and Lombard Street, was demolished in 1871.

The Coming of the Jews

1735

It was about this time that Jews began to settle in Portsmouth. They built their first synagogue in Oyster Street, laid out a cemetery in what came to be known as Jews Lane, migrated to Portsea, where they built a finer synagogue, and took a share in the good government of the town.

The arrival of Jews in substantial numbers probably coincided with their emigration from Germany, as they followed George I when he acceded to the British throne. The cemetery in question was in Southsea, and the second synagogue was in Daniel Street.

Noble and Uniform Without

1736

When Leland visited Portsmouth in 1540, he wrote: "One Carpenter a riche man made of late tyme in the mydle of the high streete a toun house." What manner of building it was there are no records to show, but of the Hall that came next, in 1736, a resident has left this description: "It is supported by stone arches, the superstructure brick containing one room and a Council Chamber, but both ill-contrived and excessive small. The outside for which, in all things, we have by much the greatest regard is indeed noble and uniform, one end being ornamented and handsome portico and the other by a Venetian window. Indeed the whole building may be well compared to the members of the Borough in their scarlet and furs, a pompous external but very small and irregular within."

This Town Hall, in the middle of High Street, lasted until 1795, when it was rebuilt. By 1836, it was causing so much obstruction, however, that a committee was formed to consider relocating it yet again. It was eventually rebuilt on the south side of the street, and became the Borough Museum later in the 19th Century.

On Guard at Southsea Castle

1739

The humorous and outspoken writer from whose pamphlet quotation has already been made thus refers to the principal fortifications at Portsmouth and Gosport:

"That old castle you see on the south side contains a very strong battery of guns, under which every ship that comes in or goes out of port is obliged to pass very near. In times of danger there is, or should be, a Governor and competent number of soldiers, but for many years past it has been kept by an old sergeant and three or four men who sell cakes and ale. As for powder and ball, our long profound tranquillity has superseded all occasion for such dangerous implements."

The same writer's description of Blockhouse Fort, Gosport's chief defence, was as follows:

"On the opposite side of this narrow water is another fort, with a row of large cannon, and a house and barracks strongly guarded by an old Irish gunner and four or five invalids — but no such thing as ammunition (except bread, cheese, small beer and gin) has appeared there for many years. The chief use it is put to is to accommodate the ladies, who come there for the benefit of the fresh sea breezes, or as a place of retirement to recover a broken constitution."

Despite the exaggerations of this anonymous pamphlet, it is known that Portsmouth's defences at this time were not strong. A French spy who later gained access to the area reported that the Portsmouth garrison consisted of a battalion of militia and a few companies of elderly or disabled soldiers who were unfit for field duty.

"The Head of Folly and the Hand of Vice"

1746

Fort Cumberland, which was in building this year, was part of the Duke of Richmond's scheme for fortifying the coast, to which an end was put by the House of Commons, the Speaker giving a casting vote against it. The fort was raised by convict labour, hundreds of these unhappy men being landed each day from the hulks, including a French prize, and then set to work according to their ability. But they were mostly unruly, there were frequent attempts to escape, and on one occasion eight men were shot before a riot could be suppressed. Gibbon, the historian, on being shown over the work, penned the following epigram:

"To raise this bulwark at enormous price,
The head of folly used the hand of vice."

Haslar Hospital

1746

The building of Haslar Hospital was commenced this year and completed in 1762. During a visit to Portsmouth and the surrounding area in 1795, Dr. George Pinckard wrote of Haslar: "The establishment is splendid and liberal and well worthy in its object; and in so amply providing for her brave and suffering defenders, England consults her best interests, while she proves herself to be mindful of the high duties of humanity."

The Port of Victory

1747

On the last day of October, Rear-Admiral Hawke came sailing into Spithead with the six prizes he had captured on the coast of Brittany, and the people went wild with joy. It was into this port that in the space of five months the flower of the French Navy was triumphantly conducted. The King honoured Hawke with a knighthood and Portsmouth added his name to the list of Freemen.

Here is an interesting as well as amusing extract from a sailor's description of the battle. He certainly had great expectations. "Such a Battell never was in all the hole world. Shot and Ball flew like hail from the Heavens. I bless God that I am still alive. In one of the Ships was found thre Milyon of Money, in the other about 16 Milyon. In all it is to be computed sixtie waggon loades of Money, and for the French warr it is all dammed for this trick, for there is ten thousand prisoners and five ships of the line, two of them are like Tours, grate ships of 90 guns. We shot the Admiril in the Ingagement; Captain Grinvell was killed. I cannot tell you half a quarter of the news. But, dear brother, this will crush the French for ever and all their desines are set on one side. If wee have justice done us, we shall have a thousand pound a man."

John Wesley's Tribute

1749

This year George Whitefield fanned the ever-increasing flame of Independency by preaching in the open air on Portsmouth Common (as Portsea was known), and a few years later "The Tabernacle" was built in Orange Street. John Wesley also visited the town and found his congregation "well-behaved, not one scoffer did I see nor one trifler." The chapel in Orange Street was built upon the ground on which Whitefield and Wesley preached.

This chapel was the mother church of the borough's Congregational churches, and the congregation grew so rapidly that by 1773 a new building had to be erected. The old Orange Street chapel was later used as a school and Sunday school, with its galleries boarded over and levelled to form a suite of rooms for needy and elderly widows. Orange Street, which ran near the present Cumberland Street, was demolished in the 1930s as part of the City Council's slum clearance programme.

The Church of the Shipwrights

1753

Not the least interesting of the documents in the possession of the Corporation is one setting forth a grant of land at Portsea for the building of the Church of St George. The grant is made to 21 people, of whom 15 are described as shipwrights. The deed states that as the parish church of St Mary is more than a mile distant, the inhabitants had agreed to build a suitable Chapel of Ease at their own expense. The Corporation, therefore, in consideration of the sum of five shillings, granted to them the site of the church at a yearly rent of a peppercorn for a thousand years.

For nearly two centuries the church stood as testimony to the faith and sacrifice of the Dockyard shipwrights. In 1941 it was badly damaged when the Germans were engaged upon their devilish work of destruction.

It is interesting to note that most of the cost of building St George's (£2,200) was raised by the sale of pews. Generations of pew-owners helped to pay for its upkeep until 1875, when it became a parish church.

Portsea is Proud of its Pioneers

1754

To the lasting honour of a few tradesmen of Portsea, the first Mutual Aid Society was formed and a system of free education established for poor children. It was known as the Portsea Beneficial Society and it continued its benefactions until 1934, when its work was transferred to the national system. Its supporters included royalty, officers of the Navy and Army, and members of the Law. Once a year its members and friends assembled in the fine hall to share in a repast known popularly as "The Pig Feast." But the children, arrayed in white, who walked in procession to St George's Church, were not forgotten.

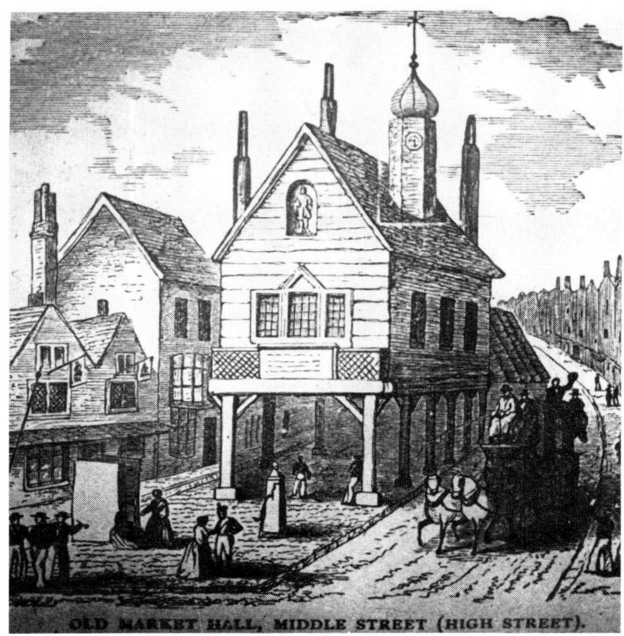

OLD MARKET HALL, MIDDLE STREET (HIGH STREET).

Gosport's Market Place

1756

At Gosport, the original market place was in the centre of High Street, a very ruinous structure of wood above which were two small rooms (in which the Lord of the Manor held his courts leet and baronial) and an octagonal tower with a clock. In 1802, the Bishop of Winchester, who was proprietor of the market place, proposed a share issue to raise money for a new one. This scheme did not succeed, but a later one did and a new market was erected, described as "a fine square building of white brick, with arched windows and bonding vaults below; and in the upper storey a large room, in which the Bishop holds his manorial court." On a flagstaff above this building were hoisted the flags by which the ferry fares were regulated.

The Execution of Admiral John Byng

1757

Portsmouth has witnessed many naval tragedies, but the one that stands out in saddest prominence is the execution on board the Monarch in the harbour on March 14th this year of Admiral John Byng, who was shot by order of court martial because he had not done "his utmost to take, seize and destroy the ships of the enemy."

The court recognised that it was confusion, not cowardice, that had led to his failure to relieve the threatened island of Minorca in the face of a French fleet. The death sentence had been passed because it was the only possible one and a strong recommendation for mercy was made. Both the King and Parliament refused to intervene, however, and the luckless admiral met his death with resignation.

The French writer Voltaire immortalised the incident in "Candide" in the following passage:

"Talking thus, we approach Portsmouth. A multitude of people covered the shore looking attentively at a stout gentleman who was on his knees with his eyes bandaged, on the quarterdeck of one of the vessels of the fleet. Four soldiers, placed in front of him, put each their balls in his head, in the most peaceable manner, and all the assembly dispersed quite satisfied. 'What is all this?' quoth Candide, 'and what devil reigns here?' He asked who was the stout gentleman who came to die in this unceremonious manner. 'It is an admiral,' they answered. 'And why kill the admiral?' 'It is because he did not kill enough other people. He had to give battle to the French admiral and they found that he did not go near enough to him.' 'But,' said Candide, 'the French admiral was as far from him as he was from the French admiral.' 'That is very true,' replied they, 'but in this country it is useful to kill an admiral now and then just to encourage the others."

In Praise of Portsmouth Beer

1757

Although the supply of beer to the Navy sometimes fell short of honest measure, the quality of the beverage supplied from Portsmouth was very good. When in command of the Channel Squadron in 1757, Admiral Hawke wrote thus to the Agent at Plymouth: "The beer brewed at your port is so excessively bad that it employs the whole time of the squadron in surveying it and throwing it overboard." He praised the beer at Portsmouth and begged that he might be supplied from that port, although he was then lying at Torbay. Sir Thomas Ridge, who was one of the leading brewers of Portsmouth, lived in a house which stood upon the site of the present Guildhall. The last use to which the house was put was that of a temporary home for the first public library.

Was it Mutiny?

1758

In January, 1758, one of the strangest and most tragic of so-called mutinies occurred at Portsmouth, when 70 men of the Namur proceeded without leave to London to lay their grievances before the Admiralty. Instead of listening to them, the Admiralty caused them to be arrested, tried by court martial, and 15 ringleaders were sentenced to death. This hideous sentence was reduced to the hanging of one man, who was chosen by lot.

The condemned men were actually on deck awaiting execution when the announcement was made that the King had decided to pardon all but one of them, and they should draw lots to see who it would be.

The Portsmouth Theatre

1759

The first theatre in Portsmouth was opened this year in St Mary's Street. Later it was removed to a site in the High Street, now occupied by the Grammar School. This was the theatre immortalised by Dickens in *Nicholas Nickleby*. Among the famous actors and singers who "fretted their little hour upon its stage" were Stephen Kemble, Edmund and Charles Kean, John Liston, Benjamin Incledon, Charles Matthews, and John Braham.

Among the many good stories told of it is that of the sailor who induced Kemble to stage, for his sole benefit, the tragedy of Richard III because he was sailing in the morning. On another occasion, the manager had enlisted a party of real British sailors to appear in "The Tars of England." As the play developed there was a fight with the enemy which became a real fight. The scene was torn to shreds, many of the "enemy" were injured, and the officer commanding them narrowly escaped with his life.

At the close of the American War of Independence, a Sadler's Wells Theatre was opened at the White Swan in Commercial Road, but it did not succeed, the cause being attributed to the alleged fact that the actors were alarmed at always finding one more person in the corps de ballet than belonged to the company.

New Landport Gate

1760

This Gate was erected this year, but for centuries there had been a fortified entrance to the town. A skeleton of the gate is still preserved, but it needs a great stretch of the imagination to visualise the many stirring events with which it is associated, the long lines of Kings and Queens, the naval and military commanders who have marched proudly beneath its massive arch. As it stands at present, an entrance to a recreation ground, it is shorn of most of its ancient beauty by the removal of the ramparts topped by massive elms and the filling-in of the encircling moats, but it retains for all who revere the past the glamour of great deeds; it brings back to the imagination the tramp, tramp, tramp of marching men, the sound of martial music, the cheers of watching thousands as the King rides past, and in the distance the bells of St Thomas ring out their peals of victory.

Landport Gate is the only one of the city's gates to be preserved in its original position, now at the top end of Warblington Street by the United Services Sports Ground.

Why a German Legion was Disbanded

1760

Upon the site of the ancient Priory of Gatcombe, Hilsea Barracks were built and the Marines were the first to occupy them when they came to Portsmouth. The barracks were much enlarged in later years, and in 1794 were for a time occupied by a German Legion, which had to be disbanded because of the serious rioting in which the men engaged.

New barracks were built in 1853, and a sizeable military presence continued there until the Second World War, when the U.S. Army occupied the site. The area has now been redeveloped as a housing estate, called Gatcombe Park. The nearby Hilsea Lines, part of the encircling defences of Portsmouth, were demolished shortly after the First World War.

How Prize Money was Shared

1762

In May of this year, the Active in company with the Favourite captured the Spanish register ship Hermione, which proved to be one of the richest prizes ever taken. The treasure was landed at Portsmouth and conveyed to London in 20 waggons, decorated with English colours over Spanish and under escort of a party of sailors. The treasure realised £519,705 and the shares of the officers and men of the Active were as follows: Captain, £65,053, commissioned officers each £13,004, warrant officers each £4,336, petty officers each £1,806, and each seaman £485.

In connection with this matter of prize money, this story will bear repetition. Just before an engagement a sailor was thought to be hiding behind a gun. Said an officer to him: "You are funking." "No, sir," replied the man, "I am praying." "What for?" inquired the officer. "Why, sir, I am praying that the enemy's bullets will be shared out like the prize money — that most will go to the officers."

A Compliment to his Admiral

1763

When Admiral Kempenfelt was about to land on one occasion, a sailor who had cast envious eyes upon a decorated waistcoat he was wearing had the temerity to ask where it was made. With a smile, the Admiral told him. A fortnight later, after the crew had been paid their prize money, the Admiral was walking down High Street, Portsmouth, when he was greatly amused at seeing the sailor who had spoken to him wearing a copy of his own waistcoat. He laughed even more hearily when the sailor showed him that the back of the waistcoat was exactly similar to the front, and exclaimed: "No false colours, sir, stem and stern alike."

The Lion and the Unicorn

1770

The ramparts and moats which formerly encircled the Town of Portsea were commenced this year. A deep and wide fosse was also cut from the Portsmouth fortifications along the side of the London Road to the Mill-dam Road, thus uniting the fortifications of the two towns. Two gates gave entrance to Portsea, the Lion Gate at the eastern end of Queen Street, and the Unicorn Gate at the western end of North Street.

Lion Gate stood at the junction of Queen Street and Lion Gate Road (now Edinburgh Road). In 1871, it was moved to become the entrance to the new Anglesey Barracks, and in 1929 it moved yet again, this time to its present site to be incorporated in Semaphore Tower in the Dockyard. Unicorn Gate originally stood a few hundred yards from its present position as an entrance to the Dockyard at the end of Unicorn Road.

The King Reviews the Fleet

1773

The visit of King George III to Portsmouth in June provided one of the most spectacular events in the naval history of the town. The presentation of the Keys preceded the royal entrance by Landport Gate, this being heralded by a salute of 132 guns. After driving through the town, the King passed to the Dockyard, being escorted by the Ropemakers carrying green boughs in their hats and wearing purple scarves across their shoulders. At the Commissioner's House, the King held a reception and conferred the honour of knighthood upon the Mayor, John Carter. In the afternoon the King inspected the Fleet, and on returning, was rowed in his barge, being followed by all the admirals and captains in their boats, the ships and forts saluting as he passed. Before leaving, the King caused more than £2,000 to be distributed and ordered the release of all prisoners confined for debt. He also set the fashion of eating Navy biscuits in the streets.

This four-day visit proved an exceptionally busy one for the King, with one of his inspections starting at 5.30 a.m. He returned for several days in May, 1778, and again in June, 1794, after Lord Howe's memorable victory over the French, when six captured prize ships were proudly displayed at Spithead.

"Jack the Painter"

1776

It was in December of this year that "Jack the Painter" tried to set fire to the Dockyard, but he only partially succeeded. He was arrested, tried, condemned and sentenced to death. On March 10th, 1777, the mast of the Arethusa, 64 feet high, was erected just within the Dockyard Gate, and to the top of this the wretched man was hoisted with a rope round his neck. His body was later hung in chains on Blockhouse Point and there it remained until what was left of it was removed by some sailors and handed over to a publican as payment of a beer score.

"Jack the Painter's" real name was James Hill, but he also went under the alias of Hind or Aitkins. After emigrating to America, he had become caught up in the revolutionary fervour of the time and convinced himself that his mission was to return to this country and destroy the dockyards at Portsmouth and Plymouth. He used a series of delayed action incendiary devices, and it was their discovery in another part of the Dockyard that led to his downfall after they failed to ignite.

Forton's Keep

1776

To secure and detain certain persons suspected of high treason or piracy, a building known as Forton's Keep was used as a place of confinement. It was from this prison in 1778 that 57 American war prisoners cleverly escaped. They first tunnelled through the wall of a cellar, hiding the excavated earth in their beds. Then they carried on to and through the outer wall of the prison and one by one crept through to freedom. To complete a good and true story, not one of them was recaptured.

A Court Martial Finding

1779

Admiral Augustus Keppel was a great favourite with the people of Portsmouth, and when a court martial found that certain charges brought against him were "malicious and ill-founded," there was general rejoicing. A famous hotel on Common Hard became known as the Keppel's Head, and a row of small houses in Portsmouth was named after him. The whole of the houses in this row were bought by the War Office in the 1860s to provide more barrack accommodation.

Government intrigue and political enmity played their part in Keppel's court martial for cowardice, the full account of which makes most interesting reading. When the verdict was announced, ships at Spithead fired salutes and a huge crowd of noblemen and naval officers escorted Keppel to his house as a hero. The Keppel's Head public house exists to this day on The Hard, but Keppel Row went sadly astray and acquired a notorious reputation until the War Office took it over.

Story of a Grand Fight

1779

Prince William Henry, afterwards King William IV, joined the Navy at Portsmouth this year and many stirring stories have been told of his daredevil adventures. One evening he entered the little inn in Tower Street and without permission drank a glass of beer which had been drawn for a young waterman, who became very angry and challenged the unknown visitor to a fight. The Prince accepted the challenge, the party repaired to Capstan Square nearby, and there the future King of England received such a trouncing that he had to be taken to the nearest apothecary to have his wounds dressed. As for the waterman, as soon as he learned who his opponent was, he discreetly disappeared. To his credit, the Prince intervened and, on promising not to spread the story, the waterman was granted a post in the Customs.

W.G. Gates said he was indebted for this story to Mr W.S. Saunders, whose father had been the apothecary mentioned.

The Royal George Sinking

1782

The sinking of the Royal George at Spithead on August 29th, 1782, was one of Portsmouth's great naval tragedies. One description of the disaster said that the ship was being heeled over so that her underwater timbers could receive attention when a mighty crack was heard, "as if the hull by some unseen force had been crushed like an eggshell in a man's hand." Orders were instantly given to right the ship, but before anything could be done, she sank "like a leaden coffin," carrying Admiral Kempenfelt and nearly all his company to a watery grave within sight of thousands who could do nothing to rescue her. The subsequent court martial found that she had been so long neglected that decay had eaten deep into her vitals, and that on the day concerned, the underwater parts of the ship had literally dropped from under her.

The Royal George took 673 of her crew with her, and remained a danger to navigation for a further 60 years before being finally removed. The ship's bell was salvaged from the wreck and is now to be seen in the belfry of St Ann's Church in the Dockyard.

High Praise from Nelson

1782

Samuel Lord Hood, who was this year admitted to the Freedom of Portsmouth, was regarded by Nelson as the "First Officer in the Service." He was a daring and brilliant tactician, a man whose burning zeal was proof against every temptation — even that of prize money. He married a daughter of Alderman Linzee, of Portsmouth, and in 1793 she was created Baroness Hood of Catherington.

When We Nearly Lost Nelson

1784

Writing from Portsmouth to Captain Locker in April, Nelson said: "Since I parted from you I have encountered a disagreeable adventure. Yesterday I was riding a blackguard horse that ran away with me at Common, carried me round all the works into Portsmouth, by the London Gates, through the town and out at the Gate that leads to Common, where there was a wagon in the road, which is so very narrow that a horse could hardly pass. To save my legs, and perhaps my life, I was obliged to throw myself from the horse, which I did with great agility, but unluckily upon hard stones, which has hurt my back and leg but done no other mischief. It was a thousand to one I had not been killed. To crown all, a young girl was riding with me and her horse ran away with mine; but most fortunately a gallant young man seized her horse's bridle a moment before I dismounted and saved her from the destruction which she could not have avoided."

Off to Botany Bay

1787

In was on May 13th this year that the first batch of convicts sailed from Portsmouth to Botany Bay, under the charge of a company of Marines, some of whom were allowed to take their wives with them. On March 24th, convicts on board one of the prison ships in Portsmouth Harbour rose upon their keepers and were not subdued until eight of them were shot dead and 36 wounded.

The fleet of 11 ships arrived at Botany Bay on January 18th, 1788, and moved on to Port Jackson (later Sydney) eight days later to establish the colony of New South Wales. On May 13, 1987, a re-enactment of the fleet's sailing was made from Portsmouth, with 11 square-rigged ships leaving Portsmouth Harbour, some of them to make the 13,000-mile voyage to Australia. A plaque commemorating the First Fleet was unveiled by the Queen at Sallyport, Old Portsmouth, on that day.

The Church of St John

1787

By Act of Parliament, a new church, known as St John's, was built upon Portsmouth Common, the site being in what is now Prince George Street. It had the distinction of being the only proprietary church in the borough, the pews being privately owned. Unhappily, this was one of the many Portsmouth churches destroyed by the Germans in the Second World War.

This spacious and elegant church, opened by the Bishop of Winchester in 1789, was destroyed by incendiary bombs in the 1941 fire blitz.

The Mutiny of the Bounty

1787

One of the most famous stories of the sea is associated with the naval history of Portsmouth. The Bounty, under the command of Captain William Bligh, was sent to carry the breadfruit tree from the islands of the Pacific to the West Indies. When the island of Otaheite (Tahiti) was reached, the sailors found it a veritable paradise, and because of this and the harsh treatment they received from their captain, they took possession of the ship and set the captain and 18 others afloat in the long boat, with a compass, sextant, and plenty of provisions. Then the captain performed the almost incredible task of navigating that boat 3,618 miles across the Pacific without the loss of a single man. When the news reached England, the Pandora was sent in search of the men and 14 were captured on Tahiti. On the voyage home, the Pandora was wrecked and four of the mutineers perished. The remainder were tried by court martial at Portsmouth and three of them hanged at the yard-arm. Another party of the mutineers had taken the Bounty to the island of Pitcairn, and 20 years later it was found that only one of them was alive. As he was leading a useful life, he was allowed to remain, and some of the descendants of the mutineers may be found there to this day.

By a remarkable coincidence, Bligh faced another celebrated mutiny — this time land-based — in 1808, when he was Governor of New South Wales. Officers of the Army corps stationed in the colony deposed him and ran it as a military junta for two years. Despite Bligh's angry demands, none of the officers responsible was hanged.

"The Golden Goldfinches"

1794

In Portsmouth and Gosport, the proposal to organise a Volunteer Force to resist the threatened invasion by Napoleon was taken up with great enthusiasm. The Portsea Battalion became known as the Golden Goldfinches because of their resplendent uniform. It consisted of a round black hat with a band of fur over it, a white feather with red top, black cockade, black stock, scarlet coat with gold wings and blue collar, the buttonholes edged with gold, the skirts edged with white and finished with gold rosettes, white waistcoat, frilled shirt, blue pantaloons edged with scarlet cord, short black gaiters and shoes. The hair was frizzed, powdered, and a tail was tied behind with black ribbon.

The Napoleonic threat led to the formation of similar Volunteer corps in Gosport, Petersfield, Havant, Emsworth, Finchdean, Hambledon and Portchester. Not all boasted such elaborate uniforms.

Signalling by Semaphore

1795

Although a station for signalling messages to ships was erected on the platform adjoining the Square Tower as early as 1569, it was not until 1795 that the first semaphore was built on Southsea Common. It consisted of a series of revolving shutters fixed in a strong framework in such a manner that they could be placed either vertically to the view of the observer at the next station, or horizontally, in which case they could not be seen. The second station was on Portsdown and there were 11 others, the last being at the Admiralty. It was no unusual experience to get a message through in five minutes, and a brief question and answer have been transmitted in a minute. In 1817, the first of the independent moveable arm apparatus was placed on the platform of the Square Tower.

The original tower on Southsea Common was replaced by a new telegraph on the Square Tower, and this in its turn gave way to one on the Rigging Tower in the Dockyard in 1833. It was from the original tower that news of the Spithead Mutiny was flashed to the Admiralty in 1797.

The Explosion of the Boyne

1795

On the morning of May 1st, a fire broke out on board the Boyne, a ship-of-the-line at Spithead, and spread with such rapidity that all hope of saving her was in vain. Her cables being burnt through, she drifted ashore near Southsea Castle, causing great alarm as the guns were loaded and shot flew in all directions. Soon afterwards, the magazine blew up with a tremendous explosion which shook the town like an earthquake. Most of the crew were saved, but about 14 people — including some wives and children — were killed.

One of the Boyne's officers, Rear-Admiral Bartholomew James, was in the debtors' prison at Portsea at the time of the catastrophe, and described in his journal how he pleaded in vain with "this iron-hearted fiend" of a jailer to release him to go to the aid of his shipmates. He even offered to let them hold his wife as a surety for his return, but this was refused. Many of the crowd who had gathered to watch the spectacle had narrow escapes when the ship's cannon discharged themselves, and several sheep grazing on the Common were killed.

The Fleet in Mutiny

1797

The Mutiny at Spithead is chiefly memorable for its happy conclusion. Conditions of life in the Navy at the time were such as to exasperate the men to the utmost pitch of forbearance. Cruelty and injustice were rife, and, failing to obtain redress by peaceful methods, the men were constrained to employ force. As soon as the Admiralty realised the serious character of the outbreak, Lord Howe was sent down with power to settle the dispute and with a Royal pardon for the mutineers. It was not long before he brought them to a sense of duty and obedience, granting them at the same time nearly all their demands. A grave crisis in the national history was thus happily averted. It was at The Three Tuns, an ancient hostelry in the High Street, that the men's delegates held their meetings, Lord Howe and other officers being kept waiting on the stairs while the men conferred upon the latest offer from the Admiralty.

Several previous muntinies should have alerted the Admiralty to the fact that Britain's seamen were desperate. For a start, their pay had not been increased for 150 years, since the reign of Charles II. They were cruelly punished for the slightest infringement, their rations were vile and frequently short weight, and leave was a luxury. The concerted, well-organised and disciplined action of the Spithead mutineers led the Government to rush through a Bill for better pay and allowances in 24 hours. Their motives were hardly altruistic, as Britain was at war with France, Spain and Holland at the time, and desperately short of ships.

The Fighting Temeraire

1798

Although Portsmouth cannot claim parental interest in the Temeraire, the famous ship built at Bucklers Hard in 1798, it is more than probable that many shipwrights were sent from this port to help in her construction, and thus a reflected glory shines upon Portsmouth. The Temeraire gained deathless fame at Trafalgar; she inspired a great poem by Sir Henry Newbolt, a splendid prose passage by John Ruskin, and a famous picture by Turner as she was towed to her last berth.

"Now the sunset breezes shiver,
Temeraire!! Temeraire!
And she's fading down the river,
Temeraire! Temeraire!
Now the sunset breezes shiver,
And she's fading down the river,
But in England's song for ever
She's the Fighting Temeraire."

Portsmouth's Gift to Nelson

1798

As there is no official record of the presentation of a piece of plate to Nelson by the people of Portsmouth, it was with some surprise and much pleasure that the Corporation accepted from the executors of the late Sir Thomas Lipton a fine silver candelabra bearing the inscription: "To the Saviour of His Country, from the Portsmouth Corporation, 1798."

Birth of the Hampshire Telegraph

1799

The Hampshire Telegraph was born on October 14th at 81, High Street, a house formerly occupied by a sea draper. It rapidly established itself as a leading commentator on naval affairs and outlived all its rivals until 1976, when publication ceased.

Sadly, the Telegraph — which provided much of the raw material for the extracts in this book — never saw its bicentenary, but during its long and distinguished life, it proved a power in the area. In 1883, it passed from its original owners into the hands of a syndicate which included Samuel Storey, a barrister and M.P., in whose family it remained for the rest of its time.

Clever French Prisoners

1799

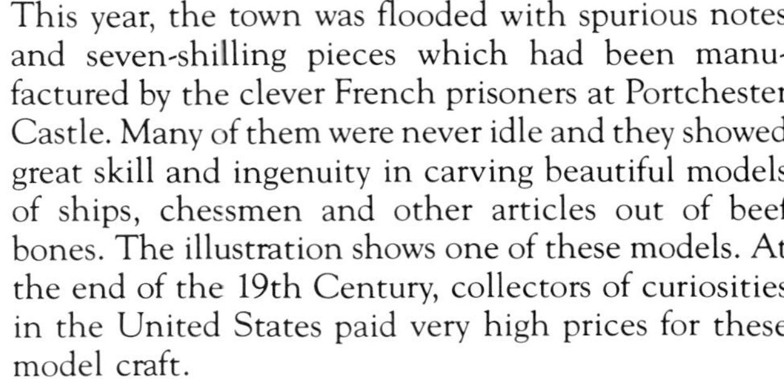

This year, the town was flooded with spurious notes and seven-shilling pieces which had been manufactured by the clever French prisoners at Portchester Castle. Many of them were never idle and they showed great skill and ingenuity in carving beautiful models of ships, chessmen and other articles out of beef bones. The illustration shows one of these models. At the end of the 19th Century, collectors of curiosities in the United States paid very high prices for these model craft.

In the years at the turn of the 18th Century, there were seldom fewer than 10,000 French prisoners-of-war confined at Portchester, the prison at Forton, or in various hulks in the harbour. Their ingenuity was not always appreciated. When they started to produce a particularly fine lace which fetched high prices, English lace-makers protested at unfair competition and its manufacture was forbidden. The last prisoners left Portchester in January, 1816, after the downfall of Napoleon.

The Merry, Merry Midshipmen

1799

In a burst of joyous existence, a number of young midshipmen fully justified Marryat's description of these budding Nelsons. One evening in November, they so plied the sentry at Sally Port with strong drink that he became an inert mass in their hands. So they tucked him up comfortably in a boat and conveyed him and the box across the harbour, landed on the beach at Blockhouse and there erected the sentry box with the still unconscious sentry comfortably within it. What he thought and said when he awoke must be left to the imagination.

Our Friends the Russians

1799

A large Russian fleet visited Portsmouth and remained for several days. A review of 5,000 troops on Southsea Common was arranged in honour of the visitors and a sumptuous banquet was given to the officers at Government House. The fleet presented a fine appearance. Some 30 years earlier, in January 1770, the Government gave permission for the crews of several Russian warships then at Portsmouth to be landed in small batches and taught by English Marines in the use of small arms, hand grenades, and other exercises.

Duels to the Death

1800

During the early years of the 19th Century, duelling was a frequent occurrence in Portsmouth. On a grey wintry morning, two officers of the Marines met behind a little lone house on Southsea Common to settle a quarrel and one of them was killed. The victor was charged with murder but acquitted "because his opponent was so irritable." Another meeting took place behind the Blue Posts in Broad Street, Old Portsmouth between two officers, and one was killed. The victor was sentenced to six months' imprisonment and a fine of £50, but was released after nine weeks.

Duels took place over the most trifling disagreements, and although several naval and military officers, with their seconds, faced trial at Hampshire Assizes in the early years of the century, all were acquitted. The last duel took place at Gosport in 1845.

Spice Island

1800

When Portsmouth was fortified with ramparts, bastion gates and drawbridges, the district known as Point was not included and the inhabitants enjoyed a number of privileges denied to residents "within the walls" of the fortified town. Among these was the right of licensed victuallers to keep open day and night, and for many years this part of the town was the nightly scene of Bacchanalian orgies and tumults. The district was known as Spice Island, either because of the bad odours through lack of sanitation or its spice-laden atmosphere as ships from the Indies discharged their cargoes there.

The less romantic version of how the area got its name is undoubtedly the true one. The stench of the Camber mud, coupled with the fact that the cesspit-emptying wagons were locked inside the town gates at night, would have given the area an unenviable aroma, particularly in hot weather.

The Ink was Long A-Drying

1800

Sir George Elliott, the elder, in a biographical memoir, relates the following: "In July, 1800, having completed my six years servitude, I was sent to London with nine other midshipmen to pass the necessary examination for a lieutenant's commission. Our examination before the old Commissioners of the Navy was not severe, but we were called on to produce certificates that we were all 20 years of age; I was 16 and four days. The old porter in the hall furnished certificates at five shillings apiece, which no doubt the old Commissioners knew, for on our return with them they remarked that the ink had not dried in 21 years."

The Ladies of Portsea Island

1801

The first census of the population, taken this year, shows the town to have been very fully inhabited, with a considerable preponderance of females. In the Old Town, the number of inhabited houses was 1,130 and the people numbered 3,148 males and 4,691 females. In Portsea, the inhabited houses were 4,180 and the people numbered 11,161 males and 13,166 females. To explain the preponderance of the ladies, the Poet Laureate Michael Drayton, who visited the town in 1598, had paid them this tribute:

"Whose beauties far and near divulged by report,
And by the Tritons held in mighty Neptune's Court,
Old Proteus hath been known to leave his finney herd
And in their sight to sponge his foam-bespawled beard.
The sea-gods which about the wat'ry kingdom keep,
Have often for their sakes abandoned the deep."

Freedom for Princes

1801

This year the Freedom of Portsmouth was conferred upon Prince William (afterwards King William IV), who was very popular with all classes. Two years later the Freedom was also conferred upon the Prince of Wales (afterwards King George IV) and, by way of giving *eclat* to the occasion, nine French prizes were brought in, including an East Indiaman valued at £20,000. The very next week seven more prizes came sailing in, to the joy of the populace.

Thirteen Years A-Building

1801

After being 13 years on the stocks, the Dreadnought was launched from the Dockyard at Portsmouth. As though to wipe out the reproach of this leisurely building, she was coppered in the short space of six hours and went out of harbour the next day. She fought at Trafalgar and ended her career as hospital ship at Greenwich.

This rose-tinted view of Portsmouth's womanhood was not shared by Dr. George Pinckard, a visitor to the town in 1795, who paid particular attention to them in recording his impressions. "To form for yourself an idea of these tender, languishing nymphs, these lovely fighting ornaments of the fair sex, imagine something of more than Amazonian stature, having a crimson countenance, emblazoned with all the effrontery of a Cyrprian confidence and broad Bacchanalian folly; give to her bold countenance the warlike features of two wounded cheeks, a tumid nose, scarred and battered brows, and a pair of blackened eyes with balls of red; then add to her sides a pair of brawny arms, fit to encounter a Colossus, and set her upon two ankles like the fixed supporters of a gate. Afterwards, by way of apparel, put upon her a loose flying cap, a man's black hat, a torn neckerchief, stone rings on her fingers, and a dirty white or tawdry flowered gown, with short apron and a pink petticoat; and thus will you have something very like the figure of a Portsmouth Poll."

This Was Portsmouth

1801

This plan, the work of a naval officer, is of special interest, as it enables one to judge the development of the island since his time. On the front was The Little Morass — little only in name, as for many years it covered a large portion of the Common. There was also a Great Morass near Southsea Castle. Milton was a very small village, the Salterns were apparently still in use, Kingston was developing around the Church of St Mary. The Portsea Poorhouse is shown near the entrance to Mill Road, and a mysterious stone marks the present position of Kingston Cross.

Salterns took its name from the salt-extracting works there which were opened up after the area was drained at the turn of the 18th Century.

Gosport as it was

1801

The people of Gosport will find much to interest them in this drawing of their town by the same naval officer. The building marked as Fortune was probably the first privately conducted hospital for sick and wounded sailors. After the opening of Haslar, it was used for the detention of prisoners-of-war. Alverstoke shows only a few houses around the ancient church, but even at this early date there was some sort of a pier at Stokes Bay.

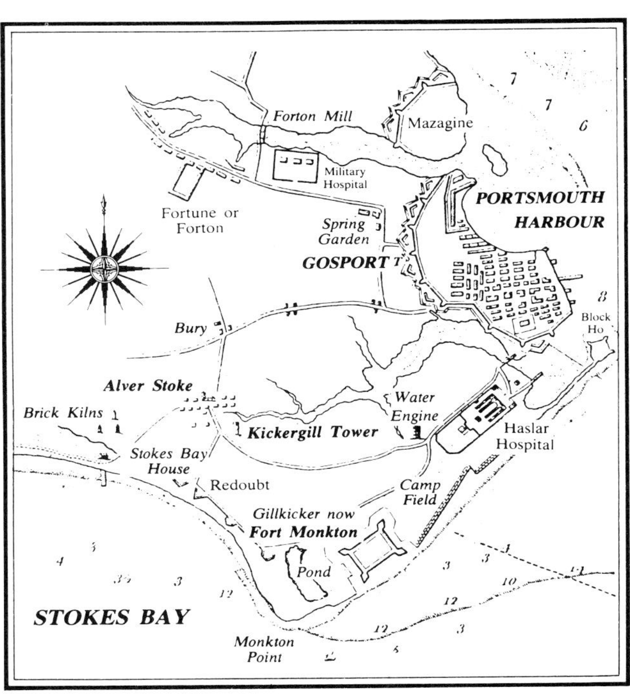

A Lover of Old Portsmouth

1801

One of Portsmouth's famous men included in the glorious company of immortals is Sir Frederick Madden, who was born in St Thomas's Street. When only 20 years of age, he published a "Study of Antiquities" and also a story entitled "Richard and Alice," founded on facts in Portsmouth in the reign of Queen Elizabeth. In 1826 he had become so well known as a research worker that he was appointed to an important post at the British Museum, where he eventually became head of the manuscript department. He took great interest in the history of his native town, and his collection of papers on the subject may now be consulted in the Bodleian Library.

When Portsea Island was a Garden

1802

The path across Elm Grove in the early years of the last century ended in a stile so dear to happy lovers. A writer at the time says that Southsea formed a plateau of cultivated fields divided by hawthorn bushes where the notes of the cuckoo were heard in May and the song of the nightingale in June. Grapes ripened in the open and cauliflowers grew to a great size.

Before its development as a fashionable watering place, the rest of Southsea did not live up to this idyllic picture. The few houses were surrounded by barren fields, and the desolate beach was littered with the flotsam and jetsam of a naval port. Stretching up to Eastney was an area known as Webb's Marshes which was the haunt of wildfowl. It was not until 15 years later that genteel Southsea began to emerge.

Beating the Water Bounds

1802

According to ancient custom, the Corporation beat the water bounds of the borough. They left in several barges, in the first of which was a band of music; in the next was the Mayor, the Aldermen in their scarlet robes, the Town Clerk and the Sergeant-at-Mace bearing the Mace, over which was flying the Corporation flag of blue silk with the crest of the borough in the centre. The procession left Sallyport and went first to the boundary post on Southsea Beach, where the Mayor, Mr. Goldson, and Mr James Carter performed the time-honoured ceremony of flogging each other round the post to impress its situation upon their memory. The boats then proceeded up the harbour and, on reaching Gosport shore, the Sergeant-at-Mace touched the shore with an oar. The Town Clerk, on behalf of the Mayor, Burgesses and Aldermen, claimed jurisdiction "in as full and ample a manner as was ever claimed and enjoyed by any of the Mayors or his predecessors."

This ceremony was repeated at several points along the shore, but it was not all plain sailing. At an official inquiry, Mr. W. Lang said there was fighting at Fareham and Gosport to prevent any landing from the boats. The people even threatened to duck the Aldermen, scarlet robes and all, if they dared to set foot on the shore. So the boundary beaters discreetly withdrew and soothed their ruffled feelings with a banquet at the Dolphin Hotel.

The Mutiny of the Hermione

1802

Passing at night through a dark passage near an inn called The Fortune of War, in order to reach the beach, a naval officer was collided with by a man who instantly apologised. Recognising the voice, the officer seized the man, dragged him to the beach, where a boat was waiting, and had him conveyed to the Guardship, where he was identified as one of the leaders in the terrible mutiny of the Hermione. He was promptly tried by court martial and within a week his body was hanging from the yard-arm of one of the ships in harbour.

The Hermione mutiny was one of a string of such uprisings which swept the fleet in the second half of the 18th Century. Her captain, a particularly tyrannical man, had threatened to flog the last man down from the mast, and two sailors had fallen to their deaths in their haste to escape such a threat. Their shipmates had overpowered and killed most of the officers, including the captain, and sailed the vessel to a Spanish port, where they presented her to the enemy. Hermione was recaptured a year later, however, and most of the mutineers were hanged. The sailor who was caught in the episode recounted above was reputed to be the ringleader.

Saving the Sailors from Themselves

1802

Sailors with pockets full of money were an obvious target for the sort of thieves and vagabonds who gathered in any naval port, particulary in time of war when there was prize money to be added. The series of Napoleonic Wars posed a special problem for Portsmouth, and by the beginning of 1802 the Mayor and magistrates decided to take steps to deal with the rising crime rate. Handbills were circulated ordering "all masters of houses of public entertainment to have a watchful eye over those brave seamen who, from inebriety, are unable to protect themselves." Similar measures were adopted at Gosport and in other ports where ships were paying off. It was not before time. As the Hampshire Telegraph observed: "We witnessed, at the conclusion of the last war, many of those brave fellows, in a few days after being paid off, begging relief as common paupers, to which they had been driven by the connivance of sharpers of both sexes." Another and happier outcome of the war was that King George III decreed that in view of their highly gallant service, the Corps of Marines would in future be known as Royal Marines, and their uniform facing altered from white to blue.

The Smuggler Who Smiled

1803

At this time, Southsea was the happy hunting ground of smugglers, whose chief resort was an inn known as The Five Cricketers which stood at the corner of what is now Osborne Road. During his boyhood days at Southsea, the celebrated writer Rudyard Kipling doubtless heard many stories of "the gentlemen," which were later incorporated into his poems.

One of the best tales told at the expense of the Customs concerned a particularly well-known smuggler who was found by an officer in the neighbourhood of Milton, where much of the illegal traffic was carried on, with two kegs of brandy in his possession. Without asking any questions, the officer seized the kegs, placed one on each shoulder, and commanded the supposedly guilty and trembling smuggler to follow him. This he did without a word, but after they had walked about three miles, the smuggler meekly said to the officer: "This is where I stop." "Oh no you don't," replied the weary exciseman. "You come along to the Custom House." "But here is my permit," answered the man, producing the necessary document, "and I am much obliged to you for your help." What the officer said is not on record.

The practice of "cheating the revenue" was almost a national pastime at this period, when the duty on all imported goods was especially heavy. It was not uncommon for supposedly respectable tradesmen to have shares in smuggling ventures, and many coastguards were easily bribed. The penalty for those who were caught was either foreign service in the Navy or an especially severe fine.

A Lesson for the Admiral

1804

Admiral Sir Roger Curtis, while travelling to Portsmouth by coach in civilian attire, found himself seated beside the mate of an East Indiaman then lying at Spithead. The stranger kindly invited the Admiral to share his bread and cheese, and then gave a long description of life at sea, not sparing many hearty "damns" at the supposed ignorance of the Admiral, who greatly enjoyed the joke. On arrival at Portsmouth, they parted the best of friends, the Admiral thanking him warmly for his picturesque information. The next morning, the Admiral, in full uniform, was walking through the High Street when he met his late fellow passenger, whom he thus accosted: "What cheer, messmate, you see I am not the lubber you took me for. But come, as I breakfasted out of your locker yesterday, you shall splice the main brace with me this evening. Then you may square your yards and run before the wind to the Motherbank." And the Admiral's command was proudly obeyed.

Mystery of a Monastery

1804

Although there are no historical records available, there is some proof that at one time in the far distant past, a monastic establishment stood on the site of Gatcombe House at Hilsea. In one of the walls could be seen the framework of an ecclesiastical doorway, and in 1877, upon the removal of a wall, a holy water stoup was discovered. It was put into use as a baptismal font in the Garrison Church at Hilsea. Further evidence was forthcoming in the discovery from time to time of human remains. At this time, the property was in the possession of Admiral Sir Roger Curtis, from whom the Government bought it for £24,000 under a defence development scheme.

"God Bless You, Nelson"

1805

In order to escape the crowd which had gathered to greet their hero as he sailed to war, Nelson left the George Hotel by the back entrance in Penny Street. The ruse was soon discovered and they quickly caught up with him on Southsea Common, struggling with each other in order to shake his hand. "I wish I had two hands," said he, "then I could accommodate more of you." The people cried out "God bless you, Nelson," and there on Southsea beach, the Admiral embarked. As the boat pushed off from the shore, people ran into the water once more to grasp that one hand and wish him God speed.

The history of the George Hotel went back to the time of King James the First, when it was a small thatched house with a water trough in front. It was known as The Wagon and Lamb. As the years crept on, the house grew in size and importance, reaching the zenith of its fame in the 18th Century, when it became the recognised resort of naval heroes, including Hood, Howe, Duncan, Jervis, Rodney, Collingwood and others. It also attracted a host of distinguished soldiers, statesmen, men of letters, poets and princes. It will always be remembered as the house in which, on September 14th, 1805, Nelson breakfasted for the last time in England. Sadly, it was blasted to ruins by the Germans in 1941.

The Gipsy's Warning

1805

Nelson had a premonition that he would never return. Mrs. Matcham, his favourite sister, who had come to Portsmouth to see him off, was wishing him farewell when he said to her: "Oh Catty, that gipsy," thus referring to a fortune teller in the West Indies who, many years before, told him that he would come to the head of his profession by the time he was 40. "What then?" he asked, and the gipsy replied: "I can tell you no more, the book is closed." The house from which Nelson's sister bade him goodbye was in consequence named Trafalgar. The Germans destroyed it in one of their bombing raids on Portsmouth in the Second World War.

When Lord Frederick Fitzclarence became Military Governor of Portsmouth in 1847, he obtained one of the anchors of the Victory which she carried at Trafalgar and caused it to be placed on the beach upon the very spot where Nelson embarked, this being a little to the west of Clarence Pier and immediately in front of the King's Bastion. At the end of the 19th Century, however, the Corporation allowed it to be transferred to its present position on the east side of the pier.

Penalties in Pride and Purse

1806

The custom of closing the town gates at a certain hour in the evening, which had been in abeyance for some time, was revived under amusing circumstances. As the town was full of military, a party of the town's proudest people waited upon the Governor with the request that he would order soldiers to keep to the road, leaving the footpaths to the townspeople. The Governor politely agreed and the necessary order was issued, but, to the amazement and anger of the "elect," they found that night and many a subsequent night all the town gates closed at 11 o'clock. No one was admitted without the password, which could only be obtained from the Town Major upon payment of a shilling. The "elect" were humbler men when next they interviewed the Governor.

Saints and Sinners are Neighbours

1806

This year a new gaol was built in Penny Street to replace the Whitehouse, the name of the common prison in the High Street, which had done service there for nearly 300 years. Prisoners were herded together there with little regard for decency, and were led in chains through the High Street to undergo their trial at the old Guildhall. In his description of the Whitehouse, Dr. Henry Slight, a local historian, wrote: "There was an underground dungeon, the descent to which was by a trap door and iron ladder, which was withdrawn at night. In this dungeon was confined the notorious Jack the Painter." The prison was only a few doors from the Vicarage

It was possible at this time to reach Portsea from the Old Town either by way of Mill Dam Road (now Burnaby Road) or by way of the Gunwharf, the King's Mill and the Mill Gate. At the end of St Mary Street it was possible to cross the moat by a small iron bridge, but carriages had to pass through the Quay Gate in order to reach Gunwharf Road.

A Promenade on the Ramparts

1809

Sir Philip Honeywood, Governor of Portsmouth in 1665, did more than anyone to make Portsmouth beautiful. He caused trees to be planted on the Ramparts, and for 200 years they adorned the fortifications. After church service on Sundays, it became the custom to promenade around the walls, and had a more far-seeing policy been adopted 100 years ago, Portsmouth would have had a unique attraction whose values would have increased with the passing years. This description of the Ramparts was written by Lake Allen, a young and gifted historian whose death at the early age of 24 was a great loss to the city:

"Portsmouth is nearly surrounded by ramparts, which are about a mile and a quarter in circumference, edged with elm trees, whose spreading foliage affords one of the most delightful promenades that can possibly be conceived. From this eminence, the beautiful view of the sea, contrasted with the landscape which the surrounding country affords, forms one of the most striking and variegated scenes imaginable."

Demolition of the ramparts was ordered as the result of a Royal Commission in 1860, which decided that the fortifications of Portsmouth were obsolete and useless. Even had they survived, it is probable that the magnificent trees would have succumbed to the Dutch Elm Disease which scourged the country in the 1970s, killing many of the fine elms on Southsea Common. Lake Allen, born in a cottage in what is now Albert Road, Southsea, brought out a new version of his grandfather's History of Portsmouth when he was only 17.

Horrors of the Press Gang

1809

Dr. Trotter, a naval surgeon at Portsmouth, wrote thus in reference to the work of the press gangs: "The scenes of cruelty and affliction which have come under my review have wrung my heart a thousand times. They are not fit to be related, for they exhibit all that is ferocious in the business of war and disgusting in the policy of a country that can permit the practice to be continued."

A quotation in the Hampshire Telegraph described a successful raid as follows: "There was a very hot press on Tuesday night by which 500 seamen were obtained. At ten o'clock at night, Captain Bowen assembled a party of Marines, with as much noise as possible, to quell a pretended riot at Fort Monckton on the Gosport side of the harbour. As the news spread, crowds ran to the fort and when the captain saw he had obtained his object, he silently placed a party of Marines at the end of Haslar bridge, the only way out, and took every man who answered his purpose as he returned from the scene of the false alarm."

One way of escape from the press gang at Portsmouth was provided by an inlet from the sea beneath a bridge at the entrance to Broad Street. By jumping into the water on the seaward side, they could swim through to the Camber and safety.

The constant need for reinforcements during years of national crisis meant that this was a particularly busy period for the press gangs. Needless to say, those who were likely to be dragged off soon found ways of fighting back. Groups of merchant seamen would defend themselves with armed sentries while they enjoyed an evening's drinking, and in Portsea, an agency flourished which provided substitutes for those pressed men who had enough money to pay a bounty.

A Family of Famous Artists

1810

Among the notable men of Portsmouth, George and Vicat Cole deserve honourable mention. Born in 1810 at a house in Pembroke Road, George became widely known by his paintings of animals. He married a Miss Vicat, of Cosham, and his son Vicat, born in 1833, developed artistic tendencies which his father diligently fostered. It was some time, however, before his skill was recognised, and it is recorded that between 1852 and 1856 he was selling pictures for sums "varying up to 40 shillings." Then came fame and one of his pictures, The Pool of London, was purchased for the nation. Towards the end of the 19th Century, the Corporation managed to buy one of his beautiful pictures, but it was destroyed when the Germans bombed the city in 1941.

Vicat Cole was elected to the Royal Academy in 1880. He died 13 years later.

"Three Buckets a Penny"

1811

Although an Act of Parliament was obtained in 1741 for supplying Portsmouth with water from Farlington, it was not until 1811 that the town was partially served from this source. Many years had to elapse before there was an adequate supply for all parts of the town, and meanwhile the poorer classes had to rely upon water obtained from wells in Elm Grove and Lion Gate Road. From these sources the water was abundant and pure. It was taken round the town in large barrels, mounted on wheels and drawn by horses. It was sold at the rate of three buckets for a penny, and the coming of the water cart was heralded by the clanging of bells.

The Rectory of Farlington was built in 1780 by the Rev. Peter Evans, who came from Portsmouth Dockyard. The church was built in 1104.

At the corner of Fountain Street there was at one time a bountiful spring of pure water, and the inhabitants came from far and near with their buckets and jars to fetch it. This spring was never known to fail. There was another at Flathouse which had the reputation of curing bad eyes.

Opposite Spring Street there formerly stood a cottage occupied by an old man and his wife who got their living by supplying the water carts from an excellent spring which was on their premises. When the road was straightened, the authorities tried to get them out, but eventually had to pay the sum they had demanded as compensation.

The early days of water supply saw competition between the Farlington Waterworks Company, which supplied from Farlington Marshes, and the Portsea Island Waterworks Company, which used a well in the White Swan Fields (near what is now Guildhall Walk) to pump 40,000 gallons an hour to homes in the High Street. The two companies merged in 1857. Portsmouth was hardly in the van of progress — it is believed to have been the last place in the country to supply water by the bucket.

The Rogue's March at Haslar

1812

In his comprehensive *History of Haslar,* the naval hospital at Gosport, Fleet-Surgeon William Tate tells an amusing story of a Governor who had exalted ideas of his importance. He required the doctors to touch their caps whenever they met him, and also expected the guard to turn out as he entered the hospital grounds. So the staff formed a lane along which he proudly passed, he was honoured by the guard turning out, and to complete the compliment he thought he was entitled to a march from the band. So they played in his honour "The Rogue's March." How the hospital staff laughed. It must have been a happy memory, especially as the Governor was unaware of the character of the martial tribute.

The Lovely Sister

1812

Gosport was described at this time as "the lovely sister of the matchless three. The country around it is pleasant, with a mild air, abounding with fine gardens and delightful walks. The neighbourhood is considered far more healthy than Portsmouth, being favoured with more land air and situated upon higher ground." The Market House in the High Street was taken down this year. In the apex stood a gilded statue of King William III.

Dickens the Immortal

1812

It was in this house in Commercial Road, Portsmouth, that Charles Dickens was born on February 7th, 1812. The novelist G.K. Chesterton later wrote: "The house is in some sense a popular shrine or memorial, enabling the sightseer to link up in one journey two of the most romantic names, associating Dickens with Portsea and Nelson with Portsmouth. All his life he defended valiantly the pleasures of the poor, and insisted that God had given ale and rum as well as wine to make glad the heart of man."

Dickens' family moved to Chatham when he was two years old, and later to London, where his experience of poverty provided first-hand material for many of his celebrated novels. His birthplace is now a living museum. He died at Gadds Hill, Kent, on June 9th, 1870.

The French Prisoners Laughed

1813

This year the number of French prisoners at Portchester and on board the hulks at Portsmouth was 9,370, and many of them were profitably employed in making trinkets and other small articles, which they sold to curious and sympathetic visitors. One night, 11 of the men on board the prison ship Vigilant managed to slip overboard unobserved. They boarded another vessel which had been left unattended and, having found some dry clothes, they fitted themselves out as British sailors, lowered a boat, and rowed to the buoy boat which was reserved for the use of the master attendant. The next step was to release her from the moorings, to raise the sail and proceed proudly out of harbour. Fortune still was on their side and they sailed over to the coast of France without so much as a challenge. Then, to crown their daring achievement, they sold the buoy boat for £700.

There were many escape attempts, both from the hulks and from Portchester Castle, where thousands of French prisoners were confined. The good ship Vigilant once again failed to live up to its name in May, 1810, when 20 Frenchmen slipped over the side. Seven were recaptured at Selsey, but the remainder were never seen again.

The Allied Sovereigns Visit Portsmouth and the Sailors Dance a Hornpipe

1814

The Treaty of Paris was signed on May 30th, and three weeks later Portsmouth gave itself up to rejoicing when the Prince Regent arrived to welcome the Emperor of Russia, the King of Prussia, the Duke of Wellington, and Marshal Blucher. The old custom was revived for the occasion. Forty rope-makers from the Dockyard, attired in white jackets and nankeen trousers, with purple sashes, and carrying white wands, met the royal carriage some distance out and preceded it to the town. At the Landport Gate, the ancient Ceremony of the Keys was performed and the Royal party passed the drawbridge amid the "most cordial bursts of welcome that ever gratified the ears of a prince."

The other distinguished visitors arrived during the day, and a special welcome was given to Marshal Blucher. Having put up at the Crown Inn, he left to join the other notable people at Government House. As he was getting into his coach, he was recognised by some sailors, who mounted to the top of his carriage and there they continued to dance a hornpipe until the destination was reached.

The next day there was a great review of the ships at Spithead, the visitors being conveyed there in a beautiful barge in which there were 16 rowers, all handsome young men in white shirts, red breeches and stockings, and black velvet shoes with silver buckles. The review, carried out in perfect weather, was exceptionally thrilling as it included the following warships captured from the French: Ville de Paris, Andromaque, Belle Poule, Cleopatre, Magicienne, and Terpsichore.

In the evening, after the review, the whole of the visitors assembled on the balcony of Government House and drank success to the British Nation. Before the Prince Regent left, he granted an audience to the Corporation, knighted the Mayor, Mr. Henry White, and left a considerable sum of money for distribution.

With the shadow of Napoleon — as they thought — receding, the Allied sovereigns were determined to celebrate in fine style. The Prince Regent scattered knighthoods liberally among naval and military officers, and bestowed a half-holiday and a week's pay on workmen in the Royal Dockyard. To complete his visit to Portsmouth, he ordered £50 to be given "to the poor debtors confined in the gaol" and a further £50 to be distributed among the poor of each of the parishes of Portsmouth, Portsea and Gosport.

The French Prisoners Go Home

1814

The clearance of Portchester began in May, 1814, and before the end of that month the 8,000 occupants of that gloomy pile had turned their backs on the flats and mudbanks of the creek. Others were hourly on the march from inland prisons to Portsmouth and Gosport, leaving the next day for France. Gradually the 18 prison ships were cleared and soon the disused buildings and idle hulks alone remained as relics of many tragic years. The brief campaign of the following year revived for a time the scenes of the past, but the end was not far off. In January, 1816, the last of the French prisoners were sent home, and from that time forward the walls of the ancient castle have looked down only on the pursuits of peace.

During their time in the castle, a passion for gambling added to the misery of many prisoners. They gambled among themselves for food, bedding and clothes, and were merciless in exacting their winnings. It was no uncommon occurrence for prisoners to go about absolutely naked. They frequently gambled away their food rations for weeks in advance and had to subsist on a halfpenny worth of potatoes which was allowed to them by more fortunate fellow prisoners.

Few weeks passed without the excitement of a duel, which was generally fought with the blades of knives or sharp pieces of iron tied to sticks. The authorities viewed these incidents lightly, but sometimes an example was necessary, and in March, 1808, a man was hanged at Winchester for killing another.

The First Steamship Comes to Portsmouth

1815

On June 9th of this year the first steamship came to Portsmouth. She was a craft of 75 tons with engines of 14 horse power, enabling her to steam at about eight knots. "The steam engine," writes Professor Callender, "invented in 1769, had been applied to vessels afloat before the outbreak of the French Revolution. Rapid strides were made with river craft, and in the year of Waterloo a sea-going ship proceeded from Greenock to London under her own steam. On her way she called at Portsmouth and the amazement caused by the sight of such a portent broke up a court martial then sitting on the Gladiator."

The Hampshire Telegraph for that date records that the vessel "produced a considerable degree of curiosity." Built on the Clyde, she was on a demonstration tour and should have towed the frigate Endymion out of harbour, but was prevented by a strong wind. Steam's rapid strides are illustrated by the fact that within eight years, advertisements were appearing for "the large and commodious steam packet Triton," which left Southampton for Le Havre every Thursday morning, picking up passengers at Portsmouth and the Isle of Wight en route. The fare was two guineas for "a spacious cabin or stateroom" or one guinea for deck passengers, with children and servants half-price. Passengers could even take their four-wheeled carriage across the Channel for four guineas.

The Endymion and her Prize

1815

Another notable event this year was the arrival of the 33-gun frigate Endymion and her prize, the American 44-gun frigate President. The British ship had 319 men against the American's 465. The fight lasted six hours before the President hauled down her colours, having lost 35 killed and 70 wounded, against Endymion's 11 killed and 14 wounded. The joy of the Portsmouth people was intense, the whole town shouting its welcome.

This incident occurred at the end of the war between Britain and America, which broke out in 1812 over the right of search on the high seas, and Britain's wish to protect Canada.

This was Real Tragedy

1818

One of the worst storms known in Portsmouth occurred on March 4th. The wind blew a hurricane from the south-west with such power that the tide rose five feet higher than the ordinary spring tides, and maintained that height three hours after it should have ebbed. As it happened, Kean, the famous tragedian, was playing at the Theatre, and three midshipmen of the Tiger at Spithead persuaded a boatman to make the attempt to land them. He tried but failed, the boat was overturned, and all hands were drowned.

A Pleasant Surprise for Portsea

1821

It was in 1821 that gas lighting was introduced at Portsea, and the promoters celebrated the occasion by erecting a lofty pedestal in St George's Square and flooding the place with light. The fate of this pedestal was rather unkind, as it was finally erected in front of Clarence Pier and used as an electric light standard. In the early days of the 18th Century, the only street lighting was from a few dingy oil lamps, and the Guardians of the Night were a few old fellows who paraded with a lantern and a stick, being paid by the inhabitants 18 pence a night in winter and a shilling in summer. The position of the Gasworks was just within the original site of the Unicorn Gate, near the end of North Street. When gas was extended to Landport, a handsome office was erected at the corner of Park Road.

A Dream That Went Awry

1822

The Arundel and Chichester Canal was one of Portsmouth's great failures. It ran from Milton to Arundel Street and was opened with great public elation. But it soon became clear that success was impossible as the sea water percolated into the soil and spoilt the well water, which in those days was the chief source of supply.

The idea of a busy trade route to London attracted many people in the early stages, and the £20,000 share capital for the canal was raised in a few days. Complaints started, however, after only two years and although traffic picked up for a time when the charges were lowered, the canal gradually fell into disuse. It was not until 1896 that a large section of it was filled in and converted into what is now Goldsmith Avenue.

The Old Order Changeth

1822

This year brought a revolution in Dockyard control, many ancient offices being swept away. They included the Clerk to the Survey, the Clerk to the Rope Yard, the Master Mastmaker, the Master Boatbuilder, the Master Carpenter, and the Master Joiner. All the Quartermen, 47 in number, were also discharged and the general establishment was reduced to 2,200 men. Much distress was caused by these radical changes.

This was the harsh effect of peace after the long years of the Napoleonic Wars. Dockyard wages had already been reduced twice, and the working week cut from six days to five. The situation was aggravated by the growing number of convicts from the hulks around the harbour who supplied a pool of free labour. Although a town meeting urged the Admiralty to stop employing prisoners in the Dockyard, nothing was done about it.

Crossroad Burials: The Last of a Hideous Custom

1823

On August 15th this year the last crossroad burial in Portsmouth took place at the junction of four roads by the Air Balloon public house at the entrance to Kingston Crescent. It was the hideous custom in former times to refuse Christian burial to the bodies of those who had committed suicide, the crowning indignity being to drive a stake through the festering flesh. To the credit of Portsmouth people, when some time later crossroad burial was prohibited, the decaying body of this suicide was taken up and re-interred in Kingston Cemetery.

Potatoes for the Poor

1823

A particularly harsh winter doubled the hardship for the growing number of families in which the husband found himself without a job. Parish relief was thought to be inadequate, and by the end of January that year, the Hampshire Telegraph had launched its own appeal in aid of the "many industrious and respectable poor families, with five, six, or seven children, in great distress." The newspaper said it knew of at least 70 such families, but estimates that there were probably as many again in the city. The figure must have been on the low side, as Portsmouth Ladies Benevolent Society had contributed to the relief of more than 800 distressed people in 1822. The appeal was reasonably successful, and raised £26 in its first two weeks, enabling potatoes to be given to 110 people, and bread and coal to the most needy. The problem was still acute, however, and the same edition which announced the appeal also told how a man had been fined twenty shillings for stealing cabbages. His companion, unable to pay the fine, was jailed for two months.

The Mystery of Kingston Cross

1823

The origin of the name cannot be ascertained, nor is it known if a cross ever stood at this spot. The name is certainly of ancient origin, as it is mentioned in the grant of the Borough to the Corporation by King Henry III. In a map of 1823 it is shown as "Stone Cross, now called Kingston Cross." It has been suggested that the name derived from "King's Stone," an ancient boundary mark at the north-west corner of St Mary's Churchyard. For many generations, the Stone was used by country people who came to service at the church, for mounting or dismounting from the pillions in which they had ridden. They tethered their horses to posts near the King's Stone.

The Coming of the R.M.A.

1824

This year the Royal Marine Artillery came to Portsmouth and were quartered at the Gunwharf until such time as better quarters could be provided. In this connection there is a good story told of the Duke of Wellington. Coming on a visit to inspect the fortifications, he made his way to the Ramparts unattended and began to wander round. A moment later a sentry approached and although he recognised the Duke, he said politely: "I am sorry, sir, but I must ask you to leave these Ramparts, as my orders are to allow no one to inspect them." The Duke, after pausing for a moment, said: "I commend you for doing your duty," and at once left the Ramparts. He afterwards complimented the officer commanding the Marines upon the action of the sentry.

Highway Robbery

1824

Public transport was frequently a risky business in the early years of the 19th Century, but it was not always highwaymen who posed the greatest menace. When the celebrated Hero stage coach left Portsmouth on a crisp winter morning in January, 1824, the four seats at the front had been reserved by four "very respectable persons to all appearances." The coachman, Francis Faulkner, knew the passenger sitting next to him quite well, his three companions were all very talkative, and the little group chattered away happily throughout the journey. At Petersfield, the coach stopped to collect a parcel of bank notes, gold sovereigns, and silver, altogether worth about £1,000, which the coachman diligently double-locked in the driver's box. The remainder of the journey passed equally pleasantly, with the conscientious Mr. Faulkner making sure that he left his seat as little as possible. As the outskirts of the capital came in sight, the four cheerful companions left the stage at various points. Arriving at the bank, the coachman discovered to his horror that there was a skeleton key in the box, which was, not surprisingly, empty. An immediate reward of £100 was offered for the apprehension of the thieves, and the coachman drove home a sadder and wiser man.

The Church where Catalini Sang

1824

St Paul's Church at Southsea was the first of two built under the auspices of the Commissioners for the provision of new churches, and soon became popular. Madame Catalini, the most famous singer of her day, gave a concert there when every seat was filled, those in the gallery at 10s. 6d. and on the ground floor at 7s. 6d. One of its most popular vicars was Henry Bircham, who also served on the Board of Guardians as the champion of the poor. Unhappily, the building was destroyed by the Germans in 1941.

Known as the Mother of Southsea churches, St Paul's stood as a gaunt ruin until 1959, when it was finally demolished to make way for a new road.

Sunday Joints Meant Shorter Sermons

1824

The second church under the scheme was that of All Saints at Landport. The first Vicar was surprised to notice how many women left before the sermon, and learned on inquiry that it was the custom in those days to have the Sunday dinner baked in the oven of the nearest baker, the time for collecting them being noon. Being a wise man, the Vicar shortened his sermons and all went well. The beautiful chancel was built in 1877 through the pious exertions of a favourite Vicar, the Rev. E.B.C. Churchill.

Designed by Jacob Owen, father of the well-known local architect Thomas Owen, All Saints was started in the summer of 1825 and consecrated three years later.

Where Artists Found Inspiration

1825

It was on April 5th this year that the first steam packet ran between Portsmouth and Ryde. As will be seen from the sketch, she was not an object of beauty, but she marked the beginning of an era of great prosperity for the Isle of Wight.

The Hampshire Telegraph took a different view of the packet, describing her as "that beautiful steam boat, the Union" and enthusing over the fact that she had made trial runs to Ryde in 34 minutes "without shewing a sail to the wind." Union transferred to the Solent from the Ramsgate to Calais route, on which she had been employed since her launch two years earlier.

Beauty and Disaster

1825

In February, the Volage of 28 guns was launched from the Dockyard, a typically elegant ship of her time. Indeed, it has been said that there was no more beautiful sight from the shore than a ship in full sail.

In September, the Princess Charlotte of 110 guns, her design being that of a lengthened Victory, was also to be launched. To witness the ceremony, a great crowd had assembled and a large number of people had taken up position on the bridge over the Dock Gates. The tide was high, and in a moment without the least warning the Dock Gates burst open, there was a terrific rush of water, the bridge was swept away, and 16 persons lost their lives.

The dead included five men, six boys, four girls, and a child of two. Seven of them were buried in Kingston Cemetery the following day, September 15th, and a public subscription was opened for the relatives. Prince Leopold led the donations with a gift of £10.

The Last of Government House

1826

This year the old Government House on the Grand Parade was taken down. The only remains of antiquity discovered were two low-pointed Saxon arches which had been incorporated into the modern brickwork, the groining still forming the ceilings of wine cellars. The walls of the mansion were three feet nine inches thick and it contained 43 apartments. The building exhibited architecture of different periods, with some lofty chimneys of remarkable shape.

Government House was rebuilt in High Street, and replaced once more in 1882 by a new building in the area now occupied by the Polytechnic at Ravelin Park. This last Government House was destroyed by an incendiary bomb in 1940.

Visit of the Lord High Admiral

1827

The Duke of Clarence, Lord High Admiral, came to Portsmouth on a tour of inspection. The Corporation proceeded in boats to the Admiralty Yacht in order to present an address, and in the evening entertained him at "one of the most splendid, costly and superb banquets ever witnessed in this, and rarely surpassed in any other, town." Such, at least, was the recorded opinion of the Hampshire Telegraph.

The next day the Duke presented a superb set of new Colours to the Marines and at great length extolled their eminent services on land and sea. The Fourhouse Barracks, in which they were lodged, were re-named Clarence in honour of the Duke.

The Marines were originally stationed at Hilsea and it was not until July, 1783, that they left that locality and did garrison duty in the Dockyard. Their headquarters were then fixed in the barracks in St Nicholas Street known as the Fourhouse. The Marines had been quartered in Portsmouth since 1753.

The Duke's visit ended with a tour of the Russian Fleet of nine sail of the line and eight frigates which had anchored at Spithead.

Clarence Victualling Yard

1828

There is no doubt that Portsmouth's loss was Gosport's gain when the entire Victualling Department for the Navy was transferred from King Street across the harbour to more commodious and more fully equipped buildings. As a matter of fact Portsmouth had such a bad reputation in this respect that some 40 years earlier, some of the more honest inhabitants appealed to the House of Commons for an inquiry. A Commission was accordingly appointed and the report ought to cause a blush on the face of Pompey even at this late day. The Commissioners found that hogs were kept upon the premises and fed on ships' biscuits, that articles from the stores were openly sold in the shop of one of the officials, that candles mysteriously disappeared, that wine was drawn in large quantities "in a clandestine manner," and that officials acted in collusion with the contractors. Can we wonder, therefore, why Gosport was preferred.

Why Was He Ashamed of Portsmouth?

1828

On February 12th, 1828, George Meredith, one of Portsmouth's most gifted sons, was born at 73, High Street; but the strange thing is that while he was alive, hardly anybody knew he was a Portsmouth man. He even went so far as to state on a census paper that he was born near Petersfield. Great though his genius was, his pride outstepped it and his family relationships were far from happy. His first and perhaps, as many of his admirers admit, his most human story was *Richard Peverel*. It was followed two years later by *Evan Harrington*, which contains many disguised references to Portsmouth and members of his own family. There remains, however, the enduring verdict that Meredith was a great genius, one of the literary beacons of the 19th Century, and a citizen of whom, in spite of his lack of respect, Portsmouth has the right to be proud.

W.G. Gates obviously took Meredith's rejection of Portsmouth to heart, because he omitted the novelist and poet from his chapter on "Some Men of Portsmouth" in his full history. Meredith died at Box Hill, in Surrey, in 1909.

Foiling the Ressurrectionists

1830

The Private Cemetery at Mile End was opened this year in order (to quote from the prospectus) "that the remains of departed friends may be deposited without the agonising apprehension of their being purloined from their silent abode for sordid gain or exposed to the dissecting knife of the medical practitioner."

Body-snatching was so prevalent at this time that night watchmen were appointed at graveyards. There was a tragic incident in Kingston churchyard in 1827 when a supposed grave robber was shot dead in a struggle in the dark. He proved to be a dockyard apprentice who had been skylarking with some friends. The Coroner's Jury returned a verdict of "death by chance medley."

The Finest Gunnery School

1830

The establishment of a Gunnery School took place this year. It was named Excellent, a Portsmouth ship built in 1799 on the lines of Nelson's Victory. She was moored so that her starboard side fronted the long extent of mudbanks in the upper reaches of the harbour. One amusing story was quoted by an admiral of the time. Every precaution was naturally taken to prevent any accident during gunnery practice, but the owner of a large house on the line of fire complained that some of the shot came dangerously near. As proof thereof, he found a large shell one morning just beneath his drawing room window, and the furrow it made as it ploughed through the sand was there for all to see. There was, of course, a devil of a row but soon all was laughter and peace when a number of young officers confessed that they had made the furrow under cover of darkness and laid the shell where it was found.

Warnings from the Past

1830

The lowest tide on record in Portsmouth occurred on March 9th of this year. The Victory grounded in the harbour, a large portion of the Hamilton Bank was uncovered, and it was possible to walk from South Parade several hundred yards towards the Spit. The brothers Henry and Julian Slight, surgeons and sanitary reformers, in their *Chronicles of Portsmouth* published in 1828, thus refer to the erosion of Portsea Island:

"The shores have been materially altered by the encroachments of the sea on the south-eastern side. Many acres have disappeared and the roots and trunks of trees which in the memory of persons now living grew on a common, are now below low water mark and are only to be seen at the lowest tides, about 100 yards to the west of Lumps Fort."

During the last 200 years, there have been many serious inundations, one carrying the sea water as far as Marmion Road. Broad Street has many times been flooded.

The Navy Does Not Forget

1834

That excellent institution, the Royal Seamen and Marines Orphan School and Home, was founded this year in St George's Square. It was afterwards removed to the Queens Rooms in Lion Terrace, and in 1876 to a fine building in St Michael's Road. The compiler of this panorama (as W.G. Gates liked to describe himself) will never forget the debt he owes to the school, to which, as an orphan boy six years of age, he was admitted, clothed, fed and taught until the time came for this transfer to the Royal Naval School at Greenwich.

The Last Two of the Town Gates

1834

The King William Gate, the least ornate of all in the city, was erected this year at the eastern end of Pembroke Road in place of the narrow Spur Gate, where on one occasion Nelson nearly came to grief. A curious feature of the new structure was that the pathway for foot passengers was so tortuous that it became known as the Crooked Arch. The entire gate was taken down in 1876 and no one mourned its disappearance.

In consequence of the extension of the Dockyard, a new wharf was provided by the Admiralty for watermen and others who had been deprived of a considerable stretch of water frontage. It was entered through the Anchor Gate, built to replace an ancient gate which marked the end of the Portsea fortifications.

The original guardhouse to the King William Gate, now called The Cottage, can still be seen in Pembroke Road. The Anchor Gate was demolished in 1897 to make way for an extension to the Dockyard.

The Great Earthquake

1834

Portsmouth and surrounding towns were severely shaken by a violent earth tremor in January, 1934, which was said to have produced "feelings of fear and awe in many persons." It came in the early hours and was even more evident in Chichester, Emsworth, Havant, and Purbrook. A contemporary account in the Hampshire Telegraph said that "the convulsive motion shook furniture and appeared to threaten destruction to the premises, the inmates becoming so greatly alarmed as to run to and fro from each other's bedrooms for aid and shelter." The paper also recalled that similar tremors had been felt in the area 20 years previously, and in October, 1734. The latter had been the subject of a paper to the Royal Society by Dr. Edward Bayley, of Havant, and had told how beds rocked, drawers and other moveables rumbled, and whole houses shook.

Portsmouth's First Paddle Steamer

1835

Great public interest was aroused by the launch in June of the Hermes, the first paddle steamer to be built at Portsmouth. She was not very big, but she heralded a new era.

Maiden Modesty

1835

At this time, maiden modesty was the cardinal rule for bathers. The ladies, robed from head to foot, descended from the shelter of a bathing machine after it had been pushed a short distance into the sea and then, firmly holding on to a rope, they bobbed up and down in the salt waves and no doubt commended themselves for their daring.

More for Botany Bay

1835

In the early years of, and well into the middle of, the 19th Century, sentences of transportation were inflicted for quite common offences, such as would now be punished by a few months' imprisonment. For stealing seven bolts, worth about a shilling, a man was sentenced to seven years' transportation. At the Quarter Sessions in April, 1835, one man was sent to transportation for life for stealing goods above the value of £5, while for stealing a pair of gloves, a girl of 13 was sentenced to seven years' transportation.

One of the first reforms of the new Town Council was to establish a police force, but the terms did not err on the side of generosity. Six street constables were appointed at £40 a year each, 12 ordinary constables at £10 a year each, and 12 night constables at fourteen shillings a week.

The sentences mentioned here were by no means unusual. At Portsmouth Borough Sessions in April, 1837, two boys aged 11 and 12 were transported for seven years for stealing a hammock, and in Sussex, a 15-year-old boy was sent to the other side of the world for a similar period for stealing bean sticks.

Government by Royal Charter Ends

1835

This year brought Charter Government to an end. The newly-elected Town Council lost no time in arranging for the building of a new Town Hall and the demolition of the Hall and Market House which had stood in the centre of the High Street for 300 years.

The first municipal election took place on December 25th, and in the evening the new members with other patriotic citizens dined at the Dolphin Hotel and drank from the Loving Cup. This cup was the one presented by Mrs. Bodkin, whose husband was Mayor in 1553. The ceremony is thus observed: the bearer of the Great Mace lowers it slightly on the shoulder of the guest who, with his companions standing on each side, has the cup handed to him and raises it to his lips and with fervour drinks to the monarch.

By the way, the writer of this note had a disturbing experience at a municipal banquet. Seated next to him was a reporter who, although a native of Portsea, had acquired American citizenship, and when his turn came to drink the loyal toast, he drank to the President of the United States. For a moment there was an amazed silence, and then came a roar of voices: "Throw him out of the window." Seeing the red light, my neighbour hastened from the room.

Portsmouth evidently passed peacefully through this reform of local government, with "not a single interruption" being recorded on that first polling day. The 42 newly-elected councillors met on New Year's Day, 1836, to choose Edward Carter as Mayor, despite his protests that his health was "not as good as in years gone by." About 50 councillors and voters dined that night at the Fountain Hotel (at their own expense), and the Hampshire Telegraph recorded that "the small hours had commenced before some of the convivial souls had left the table."

An Honoured Son of Portsmouth

1836

Sir Walter Besant, who was born in August in St George's Square, made a niche for himself in the temple of fame as one who loved his fellow men. He spent his boyhood in Portsea, and one of his many books, *By Celia's Arbour,* had many of its principal scenes based in Portsmouth. He died in 1901.

Priceless Plate

1837

Following the adoption of the Municipal Corporations Act in 1835, some ancient boroughs most unwisely sold the collection of silver plate which had accumulated during the centuries. An offer to acquire the now priceless silver which had been given by grateful burgesses was actually made by some merchants in Southampton, but the members of the newly-elected Council rejected the offer with scorn, and so Portsmouth today possesses real treasures, some of them centuries old.

The New Guildhall

1837

The foundation stone of Portsmouth's new Guildhall was laid on May 24th. The procession was led by the Band of the Royal Marines, gorgeous in white plumes and scarlet trousers. The police carried long staves ornamented with a gilt device and monogram. The building was opened in the following year on June 28th, the day of the Queen's Coronation. To mark the event a fine portrait of the Queen, painted by Swansdale, was purchased by subscription, and remained one of the city's treasures until it was destroyed by the Germans in 1941.

May 24th was the 18th birthday of Princess Victoria, and marked her coming of age. Less than a month later, she had become Queen on the death of King William IV.

The Postal Service was Humble

1838

It was in one of the houses in Green Row (now Pembroke Road) that the postal services were conducted at this time, applicants being attended to through a window open to the street. Indeed, it was not until 1858 that a General Post Office was established in the High Street. The following reference to earlier postal arrangements may be interesting. It was in June 1803 that a regular conveyance of letters to and from Portsmouth was established. The public were respectfully informed that "letters should be sent to and delivered at Halfway Houses, Kingston, Buckland, Fratton and the neighbourhood early every morning" and that "receiving houses had been fixed at the Blacksmiths Arms, Halfway Houses and the George Inn at Buckland to take in letters at one penny each, where a messenger will call every afternoon at 4 o'clock to convey them to the Post Office at Portsmouth, to be forwarded by the respective mails to all parts of the kingdom." Prior to this the rates of postage were varied with the distance, from threepence up to 15 miles, to elevenpence up to 400, and a penny extra for each additional hundred miles.

The Cobbler Saint

1839

After a serious accident in the Dockyard, which left him lame, John Pounds earned a livelihood by mending shoes. He then displayed his saintly character by carrying out a parcel of hot baked potatoes which he handed to the poorest boys of the town, and then invited them to his little workshop, where he in part clothed and fed them while inculcating the rudiments of education. His workshop, which the city wished to preserve, was bought and presented by the late Sir George Couzens but, like many other buildings, it was destroyed by the Germans in the Second World War. A marble tablet on the wall of the High Street Chapel to his memory succinctly describes his life and work.

The Last of the Royal George

1840

On the morning of May 11th, most of the people of Portsmouth went to Southsea beach to witness the last attempt to destroy the wreck of the Royal George, which had been a menace to navigation for nearly 60 years. At a given signal, a great charge of gunpowder was fired and the wreck was blown to atoms. By a remarkable coincidence, Admiral Sir Philip Henderson Durham, the Naval Commander-in-Chief at this time, was one of the few men saved when the ship sank. He was the signal lieutenant and when the ship began to sink, he managed to reach the signal halliards. In his honour, be it recorded that he directed the rescuers to help those in greater jeopardy before he himself was picked up. He had an estate at Milton and gave the site upon which the first church of St James was built.

To demolish the wreck, a huge cylinder packed with 2,400lb. of gunpowder was attached to the keel by a diver and exploded "by means of the voltaic apparatus." Immediately afterwards, operations had to be suspended because of a mad scramble by small boats to reach the mass of dead fish which had been blown to the surface, as well as a huge number of candles from the purser's store. Earlier in the week, divers had recovered two iron 32-pounder guns (one complete with its carriage and in a good state of preservation), as well as the copper-covered rudder and part of the transom with a porthole.

The First Floating Bridge

1840

A horse ferry boat was first run across the harbour in 1834. Before that time, horses and carriages had to go by road through Portchester and Fareham, this being known as "Going round the Victory." In 1838 a Floating Bridge Company was formed, and in May of this year, 1840, the first bridge began to run.

The first steam-powered bridge could carry 500 passengers and 20 carriages, and left from the end of Broad Street. The last floating bridge crossed to Gosport in December, 1959.

A Sacred Trust for the Dockyardmen

1841

It having been represented to the Ordnance Office that another place of worship was needed by the men in Government employ, a site at the end of North Street, Portsea, was given and this year the Church of the Holy Trinity began its strange career, due to the introduction of high ritual by the Vicar, the Rev. T.D. Platt. It soon became the most talked of and the best attended of all the local churches. The Dockyardmen learned to love it and when alterations and additions were needed, they carried out the whole of the work in their own time and at their own cost. Eventually the church was absorbed by the Dockyard, and it was destroyed by the Germans during a bombing raid in the Second World War.

Restored by the shipwrights in 1877, Holy Trinity was enclosed within the Dockyard in 1907 and became the church of the Royal Naval Barracks.

The Last of the Stage Coaches

1841

The birth of the railway brought death to the stage coach. Early in the century Portsmouth enjoyed an excellent service. At least 20 coaches entered or left the town daily, including the Royal Mail, the guard in his scarlet coat lustily blowing his horn. So much was this fanfare enjoyed that an actor at the Portsmouth Theatre left a sum of money to be paid to the guard of the mail coach if he blew his horn on passing Farlington Churchyard, where his body was to be buried. A blacksmith's forge formed the last link in the long trail of stage coaches, and stood in London Road, North End, until the close of the 19th Century.

Whilst ancient-minded people of Portsmouth were forecasting terrible happenings if the new system of travelling were introduced, the young and wiser generation of Gosport were making good progress with the newly-formed railway company and were justly proud when in this year the first station was opened. It was not until June, 1847, that the people of Portsmouth enjoyed their first direct communication with London.

The Home of Brotherhood

1841

Wesley Chapel, built this year in Arundel Street, achieved fame after the First World War as Walter Ward conceived and carried out a plan whereby it became the home of the Brotherhood. No sect, party, or church was recognised, but all comers were welcomed to a crusade for the amelioration of distress wherever it was to be found.

The First Omnibus Service

1841

This year the first line of omnibuses was opened in Portsmouth. It ran from Palmerston Road (then known as The Village), across Southsea Common, through King William Gate, along Pembroke Road (Green Row as it was then), through Golden Lion Lane (now Lombard Street), then through the noble King George's Gate, thence along the Gunwharf, through the Mill Gate, along Ordnance Row and Common Hard, up Queen Street, under the Lion Arch to Commercial Road, and thence to North End. The fare was sixpence all the way.

The Church of the Runaways

1841

On the afternoon of September 30th for the first time in Milton was heard "the Vesper Bell so full and swelling." It announced the consecration of the Church of St James, which had been erected by public subscription, the site having been given by Admiral Sir Philip Henderson Durham. It was only a little church, but perhaps the lovelier for its lowliness. It soon became known as "The Runaways' Church," as lovers from other parishes were allowed to marry there. A grander edifice now occupies the site.

The present church in Milton Road was built in 1913, a short distance from the original.

The Saving of Southsea

1842

To lessen the danger of coast erosion and provide a pathway along the shore, Clarence Esplanade was constructed this year. The War Department gave the land and convicts were employed in bringing thousands of tons of mud and shingle from the Dockyard, where the steam basin was under construction. The Esplanade was opened during the Royal Portsmouth Regatta, which was attended by the Queen, the Prince Consort, and other members of the Royal Family. During the Crimean War, Queen Victoria reviewed a large number of wounded men in the Dockyard, and wept as they were carried by trying to sing the National Anthem. After the war, she presented the Victoria Cross to 12 officers and men on Southsea Common.

Victoria Pier, the first of its kind, was constructed this year, and for some years was a most popular resort. It took the place of the old Beef Stage, from which the Fleet was provisioned.

The pier was washed away by heavy seas during a storm in 1925, and a new one built by the council five years later. The building of the esplanade was one of the first acts of Lord Frederick Fitzclarence when he became Governor of Portsmouth. It was named after his father, the Duke of Clarence, who had remarked 20 years earlier that an admirable promenade could be made along Southsea Beach.

The Grog was Very Good

1842

The first Naval Review by Queen Victoria, in February, 1842, was a very small affair, but there were several interesting incidents connected with it. Having been taken round the Fleet in the yacht Black Eagle, she went on board the Queen, the first three-decker built at Portsmouth in her reign. She found the men at dinner and as they rose on her approach, she begged them all to be seated and "carry on." She then desired to taste their grog, and the captain gave orders for a glass to be brought, but she said she wanted to drink it just as the men did, from a metal pannikin. So thus she tasted it and declared it to be very good, as proof thereof taking a second sip. She also tasted the men's soup, and so delighted were they that they gave her the biggest cheer she had ever known. And thus she replied: "I feel today that I am indeed old Ocean's youthful Queen, surrounded by those who will uphold that title in the Battle and the Breeze."

The landlord of the Globe Inn, a Mr. Sartain, was not so fortunate on this occasion. At only one day's notice, he had provided a fine spread in the Admiral's cabin, but when Her Majesty was invited to take refreshments, she declined.

The First Church of St Mary Goes Down to Dust

1843

As the first church of St Mary had outlived its usefulness, a second building was erected this year. It had nothing to distinguish it and the interior was of a most depressing character. It was not only lacking in light and ventilation but many of the congregation could not even see the east end of the church or the preacher. It was short-lived, as later records will show. When removing the foundations of the old church, a stone coffin was discovered close to the altar. It bore no date or inscription except the Crusader's Cross prominently carved upon the whole length of the coffin lid. It is thought to have contained the body of some dignitary who had served in the Holy Wars and must have been buried between the 11th and 13th centuries. In the view opposite of the second church, it will be seen that the tower of the first was left standing.

The original plan was to rebuild the church on the opposite side of the road, but it was rejected as too expensive. Instead, Thomas Owen grafted a replacement church on to the medieval tower, a bizarre marriage of styles that continued until the present church was built. The foundation stone was laid in 1887 by the Empress Frederick of Prussia, eldest daughter of Queen Victoria, and the church was consecrated two years later.

The Last King Visits Portsmouth

1844

In October, Louis Philippe, the last King of France, escorted by a small squadron of warships, visited Portsmouth. As the Royal Yacht entered the harbour, salutes were fired and the flags of the two nations waved side by side. When the Mayor and Corporation went on board to deliver an address, the King smilingly told them that he knew Portsmouth well and had stayed at the Fountain Hotel. Before leaving, the French Squadron was reviewed by Queen Victoria.

The Castle a Prison

1844

Much to the annoyance of residents of new Southsea, the Castle was converted into a military prison. It was an entirely undeserved humiliation after its 300 years of national defence, and also a reproach to the new community growing up on the other side of the Common.

The Last Fatal Duel in England

1845

The most sensational duel in our local annals, and happily the last, was between Lieutenant C. Hawkey, of the Royal Marines, and Captain A. Seton, of the 11th Dragoons. The place of fashionable assembly at this time was the King's Rooms on Southsea beach. It was there that Captain Seton met Mrs. Hawkey, and though he had a wife of his own, he paid her marked attention. At length Mrs. Hawkey complained to her husband and, after a dance at the King's Rooms, he called Seton aside and threatened to horsewhip him down the High Street if he did not accept his challenge to a duel. After some hesitation, Seton agreed. The meeting took place at Browndown and Seton was mortally wounded. Some time later Hawkey was put on trial at Winchester for murder, and was acquitted because of the provocation he had received. This duel created a great sensation throughout England, and from that day this barbarous practice has been banished from English society.

An Historic Duel

1845

This year a duel took place at Spithead to determine the respective merits of the paddle and the screw. As recorded by the Morning Post, the duel was between the Alecto and the Rattler, two ships of exactly the same tonnage and power, Alecto being a paddle ship and Rattler having a screw. They were secured stern to stern and ordered to go full speed ahead. The result was that Alecto, churning madly but impotently, was towed quietly away, stern first, at a speed of two and a half knots by Rattler with her screw. So the propeller came into its own.

A Royal and Sorrowful Farewell

1845

A Review at Spithead this year by Queen Victoria is memorable because of the last brave and beautiful farewell of the sailing warship. The fleet went through the evolution of "making all sail" and then shortening it, sail by sail, until they were under close-reefed topsails. As the Queen passed, officers and men stood silently and sadly at the salute.

The Hospital is Built to Serve and Save

1847

Although many efforts were made in the early years of the last century to provide medical and surgical aid for the poor, it was not until 1846 that a movement was set on foot for the establishment of a fully equipped hospital. The Board of Ordnance showed the right spirit by granting at a peppercorn rent for a thousand years the site upon which the hospital was built. On September 27th, the foundation stone was laid by the Prince Consort.

This building was the Royal Portsmouth, Portsea and Gosport Hospital, later abbreviated to the better known name of "the Royal." Part of it was badly bombed during the Second World War, but it survived until 1979, when it was closed. The hospital was demolished in 1984, but some particularly fine panels of tiles depicting nursery rhyme scenes, and originally mounted in the children's wards, are preserved in Portsmouth City Museum.

Where Sovereigns Would Tarnish and Silver Turn Blue

1847

This year a terrible cholera scourge swept over the town, causing many deaths. Sanitation was almost unknown, and it was a common saying that "in Gold Street your gold would tarnish, in Silver Street your shillings would turn blue, and in Copper Street your pennies would be covered with verdigris." But the epidemic served a useful purpose, as the Town Council at once put the Public Health Act into operation and from that day Portsmouth began to adopt those sanitary reforms which have converted the city into one of the healthiest places in the land.

The epidemic raged through the filthy and overcrowded streets, and returned even more violently in the following year, killing an estimated 800 people. There was no public sanitation to speak of, and one well-known doctor described Portsea Island as "one large cesspool." Nor were matters improved by the fact that no two medical opinions could agree on the cause of cholera.

The Purification of Point

1847

This year there was a clearance of 19 houses on the western side of Broad Street, the site being needed for the completion of the fortifications. Describing this interesting event, Dr. Henry Slight wrote as follows: "The first blow has been struck at the Blue Anchor, where the voice of the violin was never silent. As a lad I have been in these defiled rooms to deliver messages and parcels to the captains' coxswains, and have been paid bills from the apron of the landlady, held over her arm and filled with the coinage of every part of Europe. The complaints were eternal to the authorities of sailors who, in a few hours in sleeping rooms to the rear, had lost the whole of their pay and prize money. On the first floor of the house was a cockpit, where large sums of money were lost and won."

The extension of the Dockyard involved the acquisition of an entire district known as "The New Buildings." It was a little township in itself, enjoying all the amenities of the time. It had a brewery of its own, a bowling alley, and a place of assembly proudly known as "The Parade." Once a year the inhabitants elected a mock Mayor, who sat in state on the Parade as a local and unique company known as the Royal Snuffs marched by. The day closed with a great bonfire on the site of what came to be known as Bonfire Corner.

The End of Free Mart Fair

1847

After a life of more than 600 years, Free Mart Fair was abolished by Act of Parliament, much to the relief of law-abiding citizens, as it had degenerated into a fortnight's saturnalia. Anciently, it was of great importance, as it became a mart for the sale of woollen goods and was much resorted to by the French from Normandy, and the Dutch. During the period of the fair, it was the custom to display an open hand as expressive of the welcome which strangers might expect to receive. The hand was stolen in 1840 and reported to have been taken to America.

The problems of the fair are typified by a report to the Commissioners for England and Wales in 1835, which stated: "Disreputable characters of every sort haunt the town during its continuance, and the streets are in a state even more disorderly than usual. Many of the inhabitants quit Portsmouth for the time to avoid the nuisance." Nine years later, the Hampshire Telegraph reported: "We never recollect a larger influx of vagabonds than have followed in its wake on this occasion, or so much disorderly conduct at night." To continue the historical tradition, a one-day version of the fair was revived in the 1970s — but free from saturnalia.

Portsmouth's Loss is Gosport's Gain

1848

The Marines first came to Portsmouth in 1755. They were stationed at Hilsea, and it was not until 1783 that they left that locality and did duty in the Dockyard. Their headquarters were then fixed at the Fourhouse Barracks in St Nicholas Street. This year they were transferred to Gosport, the alleged reason being the inability of the Lieutenant-Governor, a son of William IV, to include them in the military displays which he so much enjoyed, the Marines being under the jurisdiction of the Admiralty.

No Doubt the Great Heroes Approved

1850

Before giving up his command as Lieutenant-Governor, Lord Frederick Fitzclarence wrote to the Town Council expressing the wish to present "statues of our immortal heroes Wellington and Nelson. With the glories of both this town may be said to be connected, as from the beach Lord Nelson left to conquer and die at Trafalgar, and the Duke sailed from this harbour to conduct that great war of the Peninsula which conduced so signally to promote the peace of Europe."

On June 18th, the statues were unveiled on Southsea Common in the presence of 50,000 spectators. But, alas, they came to an untimely end, as the salt spray cast up by the sea caused the stone to crumble, and they became such an eyesore that one night a naval officer with his boat's crew hauled the perishing statues from their pedestals, carried them to Spithead, and committed them to the deep.

Had Lord Frederick lived to hear of this sorry ending to his patriotic gesture, he would doubtless have caused other and more permanent statues to be made, but he died in India in 1854. Before leaving, he had put aside £50 a year for the poor of Portsmouth. He did real and lasting service to the borough, and is gratefully remembered.

Lord Frederick succeeded his father, the Duke of Clarence, as Governor in 1847, and it is after them that Clarence Esplanade at Southsea is named. The statues were unveiled on the anniversary of Waterloo, but the day was an inauspicious one all round. The Hampshire Telegraph reported: "By a strange mismanagement, the Common was let off into gingerbread stalls, shows, and very many beer shops, and Tuesday, with its night, and the following day and night exhibited more drunkenness and indecency than we ever remember to have seen." The gentry were no better, for at the official dinner in the evening, political insults were traded with one of the town's two M.P.s, Sir George Staunton, and the Telegraph could only presume "that as the day was extremely hot and everybody had been a long time in the sun, a few sips of wine speedily overpowered their reason."

Eight Warships in a Decade

1850

During the decade 1850-59, Portsmouth Dockyard was extremely busy, no fewer than eight warships being launched. Details of these can be found in the *Naval History of Portsmouth.* In 1850 a new graving dock was opened and the Furious, a paddle frigate, was launched. In 1852 the Princess Royal, a 91-gun ship, was set afloat. The Marlborough, of 131 guns, should have been launched on August 1st, 1855, but she refused to take to the water until the following morning, when the launch was completed by the united exertions of 2,000 men. In November the Shannon of 51 guns was launched, and she added a splendid note to naval history during the Indian Mutiny. In 1857 the Royal Sovereign was launched and to crown the decade, the Victoria, of 121 guns, was launched in the presence of the Queen whose name she bore. Then came the Duncan, 121 guns, and finally the Bacchante, of 51 guns. As a footnote to this brilliant record, a Dockyard Volunteer Regiment was formed for the protection of the Yard.

Honouring St George's Day

1851

The Royal Sailors Home in Queen Street was opened on St George's Day with appropriate ceremony. A start was made with 30 beds, which number was increased to 90 by the end of the year. In 1855 the Prince Consort visited the Home and was so pleased with all he saw that the Queen became a Patron and sent £500 to extend the accommodation. In 1870 the number of cabins was increased to 273. Five years later further additions were made and the directors were fortunate in being able to acquire the adjoining Fighting Cocks Tavern, which had hitherto caused difficulties in the management of the home. The next addition was the Jubilee Wing in 1887. Ten years later, another large wing was built, at a cost of £10,000, and in 1907 the King Edward VII Wing was opened. During the 1914-18 war the Home prospered greatly, the whole of the debt was wiped off and the constitution so changed that it became, in the best sense of the word, a well-appointed and well-conducted seamen's club.

Praise for the Bumboat Women

1852

Handsome tributes were paid to the bumboat women who, in spite of the weather, went out to Spithead with fresh bread and meat for the homecoming crews. But all were not as innocent as they looked. Bringing liquor on board was strictly forbidden, but one woman contrived to secrete under her petticoat a number of bladders filled with spirit. After being emptied on board they were inflated so as to preserve the rotundity of the lady's figure, and this was her undoing. One day, after leaving the ship's side, the boat was capsized in a sudden squall and the way in which that lady rode the waves was a wonderful sight for the men who rescued her, until the hidden bladders were revealed. She went ashore a sadder and wiser woman.

The Wreck of the Birkenhead

1852

On January 2nd, the troopship Birkenhead left Portsmouth and on February 26th, she was wrecked off Danger Point, South Africa, 436 lives being lost. The behaviour of the troops forms one of the noblest pictures of British history. After the women and children had been placed in the boats, the word was given to all hands to save themselves. But the officer in command of the troops who had drawn up on deck as though on parade, realising that a rush to the boats would imperil the lives of the women and children, gave the order "As you were." Not a man moved. They went down with the ship but left us a deathless story.

"There rose no murmur from the ranks,
no thought,
By shameful strength, unhonoured life to seek;
Our post to quit we were not trained, nor taught
To trample down the weak.

So we made women with their children go,
The oars ply back again, and yet again;
Whilst inch by inch, the drowning ship sank low,
Still under steadfast men

What follows why recall? The brave who died,
Died without flinching in the bloody surf;
They sleep as well beneath the purple tide,
As under other turf."

Despite the undoubted bravery of the troops, the scene must have been one of dreadful confusion. It was two hours after midnight when the Birkenhead struck a rock in smooth seas, and she went down in 20 minutes. Many of the men asleep below decks were drowned in their hammocks. One infantry lieutenant who spent five hours in the water reported later than many people escaped the sinking ship only to be taken by sharks. An interesting sidelight on communications at the time is the fact that news of the tragedy took nearly two months to reach Britain.

Funeral of General Sir Charles Napier

1853

On August 14th, the body of General Sir Charles Napier was interred near the entrance to the Garrison Church. The funeral is said to have been the most impressive ever seen in Portsmouth, with a crowd estimated at 50,000 lining the streets to watch the procession. General Napier, the conqueror of Scind and former ruler of that Indian province, died at his home at Oaklands, Purbrook. Napier Road in Southsea commemorates his name.

The Military Hospital

1853

This hospital in Lion Terrace, Portsea, was built on the site of extensive wooden barracks which had been used during the Napoleonic Wars. At the close of the 19th Century, the building was transferred to the Admiralty, who provided in lieu the Alexandra Hospital on Portsdown.

Queen Alexandra Hospital was originally used as a home for those disabled in the First World War. Bomb damage in 1941 to the Royal Portsmouth Hospital forced the transfer of the first civilian patients to "Q.A.", as it is affectionately known. A major expansion took place in the 1970s after the Royal Hospital was closed.

First Review of Steam Warships

1853

The first Royal inspection of a fleet of steam warships took place at Spithead on August 11th and attracted extraordinary attention. There was a great rush of people to Portsmouth to witness the review, and all through the preceding night the streets were crowded with hapless visitors in search of a bed. Of the 22 ships in the line, 13 were screw steamers and nine were propelled by paddles. After the Royal Yacht had passed down the line, the signal was given to proceed to sea. The fleet was then divided into two squadrons, the ships cleared for action and a mimic battle ensued, much to the gratification of all beholders.

The new steam engines certainly drew immense crowds. Hundreds of people spent the night sleeping on benches on the piers along the harbour, and the Hampshire Telegraph reported that "one canny housewife scraped together about a score of Windsor chairs, which she placed carefully round a good-sized apartment and let rapidly at five shillings a head."

A Charnel House

1854

This picture of the churchyard of St Thomas as it was when a reform of the Burial Laws was enforced, gives a faint idea of the mass of corruption which not only surrounded the church but was heaped beneath its floor. The number of bodies interred during the 700 years of the church's existence can only be conjectured, but it must have run into many thousands. Although intra-mural burials ceased in 1854, the clearing of the ground beneath the church was not undertaken until the beginning of the present century, when the Vicar, the Rev. Charles Darnell, undertook the cleansing of the Augean stable and sacrificed his own life in the work.

When the Marlborough Paused

1855

The Marlborough, of 121 guns, was in the process of being launched from Portsmouth Dockyard when, to the amazement of all beholders, she slowly brought up when two-thirds out of the shed and remained immovable on the ways, the bows remaining in the shed and the outer body in the Harbour. So unlooked-for a casualty took everybody by surprise, and the enthusiasm which greeted her start subsided into silence. The ship remained fast until the next tide, a little after midnight, when the launch was completed by the united efforts of 2,000 men. Her end was equally sensational, as in 1924 she sank in the Channel on her way to the shipbreaker's yard.

An earlier ship of the same name had been even more unlucky. After a gunpowder explosion ripped through H.M.S. Marlborough in Portsmouth Harbour in 1776, killing 18 people, the Gunner was sentenced to a year's imprisonment for carelessness.

The Glorious Peace Review

1856

At least 600,000 spectators witnessed the Peace Review of 1856. The scene was magnificent. A violet sky, pure and unclouded, the rippling sparkling sea, the white sails of the numberless yachts and other vessels, the ceaseless flow of steamers, the hum and flutter of the multitude formed a sight as gay and brilliant as any ever witnessed from British shores. But it was not without its amusing side. By some strange blunder, the Members of the Houses of Parliament were sent by rail to Southampton instead of Portsmouth, and there was no tender there to carry them to Spithead. When at last they were conveyed to the great display of more than 250 ships, no notice was taken of them. They were treated as outsiders, and to crown their misfortunes the train that took them back again was so delayed that they were landed at Waterloo Station at four o'clock in the morning, whence bishops, judges and politicians had to find their way home on foot.

It is ironic that the mismanagement which marked the Crimean War's military campaigns should have extended to the Peace Review on April 23rd that year. Even Cabinet Ministers and diplomats were not immune from the chaos. The cabs and omnibuses which had been reserved to take them from the railway station to Southsea Common were "hijacked" by a clamouring crowd of Londoners who had come down for the celebrations. When the Prime Minister, Lord Palmerston, arrived and learned of this he was at first annoyed, but later admitted that "it was quite right to give way under the circumstances."

Where the Ghost Walked

1856

The Theatre Royal in Commercial Road was opened this year by Mr. Henry Rutley. It was built upon the site of an old racquet court which had been used for a variety of entertainments, including dramatic performances, but these latter were abandoned because the performers averred that there was a ghostly addition to their company at the close of each performance. Mr. J.W. Boughton, one of the most genial of men, succeeded to the management and raised the theatre to the height of its dramatic fame, and Mr. Peter Davey, who followed, made gallant and prolonged endeavour to maintain its noble reputation. Then came the moving pictures, and lovers of the glorious company led by Shakespeare had to wait until the new order changed again.

The Cambridge Barracks

1856

These barracks in the High Street were built this year, the clearance of the site involving the demolition of a number of ancient private dwellings as well as the old theatre immortalised by Charles Dickens in "Nicholas Nickleby." The Rampart was still in position, and it was possible at this time to traverse it in rear of Penny Street, St Nicholas Street and Barrack Row, then to cross over King William Gate and continue a glorious promenade to the Grand Parade. It grieves one to imagine what Portsmouth has lost in beauty by the sacrifice of these incomparable promenades.

The barracks continued in military use until 1926, when they were taken over by Portsmouth Grammar School.

The Victoria Cross

1858

There was a glorious company on Southsea Common on the afternoon of August 2nd to witness Queen Victoria present to 12 officers and men the Cross bearing her name, the highest and most prized reward for exceptional bravery. The whole of the troops in the garrison were present at the parade, and 20,000 of the people of Portsmouth greeted the Queen.

Portsmouth had been the scene of constant sailings and arrivals during the two years of the Crimean War, at first full of bands and brave cheering, later in more subdued vein as shiploads of sick and wounded men returned. A Crimea Monument was erected on Clarence Esplanade in June, 1857, by the Debating Society of Portsmouth.

A Record in Church Building

1858

The strange structure shown here was built in the space of four weeks as the first Church of St Bartholomew at Southsea, and soon became known as the Crinoline Church. It later served as the first Church of St Simon, and was next removed to Eastney, where it became the temporary church of the Royal Marine Artillery.

This unique structure cost only £600 and began its life in Outram Road to serve a congregation while the permanent St Bartholomew's was built. In 1862 it was re-erected in Waverley Road as the temporary St Simon's Church, and after a further four years moved to the Royal Marines Barracks. It was demolished in 1905.

The Smuggler's Ruse

1860

This record of local smuggling would not be complete without mention of a novel and disconcerting experience which once befell the Rev. F. Baldey, Vicar of St Simon's at Southsea. One day a huge parcel was delivered at the Vicarage, and upon opening it, the Vicar, instead of finding books as he expected, discovered a quantity of tobacco, many pounds in value. As he was a law-abiding citizen and a non-smoker to boot, he promptly communicated with the police, who were thus able to unravel a very clever smuggling system. The contraband goods were packed at a distributing station, addressed to men of the highest respectability, and sent by train. At the railway station, confederates were waiting to collect the parcel, having been sent for that purpose. On this occasion, however, they arrived too late to find, much to their chagrin, that the parcel had been despatched to the Vicarage by the ordinary railway delivery van.

Two Famous Engineers

1859

Isambard Kingdom Brunel was born at Portsea on April 9th, 1806, and in his early youth displayed an aptitude for the profession of his father, who was the inventor of the block machinery in the Dockyard and which for years was the chief wonder of that establishment, not being improved upon for a century. The chief works of Isambard were the suspension bridge at Clifton, the great bridge at Saltash, the Box Tunnel (at the time the longest in the world), the broad gauge of the Great Western Railway, the building of the Great Western in 1838, the first regular liner between England and America, doing the voyage in 15 days, and the building of the Great Eastern, a vessel of 12,000 tons with accommodation for 4,000 passengers. Among other great services, Brunel introduced the screw propellor in large steamships, and through him it was adopted in the Navy. The Great Eastern was too much for him, and the day of her trial trip, September 5th, 1859, he broke down. Ten days later he died, at the age of 53. His memorial may be seen on the Thames Embankment.

Palmerston's Folly

1860

In earlier times, the mothers of Portsmouth used to quiet refractory children by telling them that "Boney will take you." The fear of a French invasion was still strong 50 years later, and so impressed the Government at this time that nearly two million pounds were spent in providing more or less useless fortifications — five forts on Portsdown, the rampart and moat at Hilsea, and five fortifications in the Solent. The whole scheme became known as Palmerston's Folly, possibly without justification.

This immensely expensive scheme made Portsmouth one of the most strongly defended towns in the world, but was just about the last example of the dying practice of throwing a ring of forts around the area to be protected. The era of the long-range shell, both on land and sea, was just around the corner. Whether it was folly to build them or not, Lord Palmerston and his Cabinet soon found that their magnificent defences were obsolete.

Camber Development

1860

Having resolved still further to develop the Camber, the Town Council obtained an Improvement Act under which a dry dock was constructed and other improvements effected. A swing bridge was replaced by a bascule, or lifting bridge, but this was removed in 1907 to provide more wharfage accommodation.

"Black Charlie" is Honoured

1860

By this name Admiral Sir Charles Napier was known in the Navy, in which he was a special favourite with the men whose interests he always studied. His death this year led to the erection of a memorial, now in Victoria Park but originally placed at the junction of Commercial and Edinburgh Roads.

The Home of the Royal Marines

1860

As early as 1539 a fort was constructed on the shore at Eastney, but it was not until this year that barracks were built there for the Royal Marine Artillery. In 1923 they were joined by the Royal Marine Light Infantry from Gosport, and the two famous Corps were amalgamated under the title of Royal Marines.

The barracks are now largely empty and the fate of the buildings and land has yet to be decided, but the magnificent officers' mess has been preserved as a splendid Royal Marines Museum, which tells the 300-year history of the Corps.

One of the Healthiest Cities

1860

Portsmouth should bear in grateful remembrance the services of the Slight brothers, both surgeons of repute and both local historians. At an inquiry into the sanitary condition of the borough, they helped materially to set the authorities upon the path of reform, the result being to make Portsmouth one of the healthiest cities of the land.

Clarence Esplanade Pier

1861

This pier, which was opened in June, contributed in bounteous measure to establish the popularity of Southsea as a health and pleasure resort. Horsed tramcars ran on to it from the railway station with passengers for the Isle of Wight. Some years later the experiment was tried of promenade concerts at a uniform charge of sixpence, and they proved an unqualified success.

Music played a large part in the early life of the pier. On one Sunday shortly after it was opened, more than 1,000 people paid for admission (as well as many who got in free), and a few days later, the band of the 5th Hants Rifle Volunteers performed its new set of Esplanade Pier Waltzes to an admiring crowd. The formal inauguration did not take place until early July, when the toll houses and refreshment rooms were complete. The pier was bombed during the Second World War, and re-opened in its present form in 1961.

Last of the Commissioners

1861

The Commissioners' Hall in Arundel Street, which had been built to the fading glory of the Landport and Southsea Commissioners, was opened on May 7th with due ceremony. To celebrate the event, the Commissioners gave a dance in the Great Hall to their friends, and in order to assert their rights, the public forced their way in a few nights later and made merry until the sun rose in the morning.

Whale Island

1861

Until 1845 Whale Island, in the upper reaches of the harbour, was covered at every spring tide and presented the appearance of a whale's back, hence its name. By successive deposits from excavations from the Dockyard, the surface was raised several feet above sea level. This year the Admiralty bought it with the object of converting it into a naval training station. They gave the Corporation £1,000 for it, and then Winchester College claimed ownership and wanted the money. The law was invoked and after spending about £200, the two claimants agreed to share the remainder of the money. Whale Island was further improved and became one of the finest naval gunnery training centres in the world.

The Portsmouth Police

1862

Soon after the passing of the Municipal Corporations Act in 1835, a Police Force was appointed with a superintendent at £100 a year and a house, three inspectors at £30 per annum, three sub-inspectors at 17 shillings a week, with court fees equally divided between the six. There were 24 constables at 17 shillings per week. The Force was to be clothed by the Watch Committee, but deductions were made from pay until the cost was liquidated. Whether the Council prided itself upon its wisdom and generosity is not on record, but as the town advanced in size and importance, the Police Force was gradually raised to full strength necessary to maintain law and order.

An Abominable Nuisance

1861

The idea of sheep and cattle in Old Portsmouth may sound delightfully rural today, but was regarded as a thorough nuisance by residents of mid-Victorian times. The narrow streets were frequently full of animals being driven to various slaughterhouses in the neighbourhood, including the military one. By the beginning of 1861, these noisome neighbours had become the subject of frequent complaints to the Town's Commissioners, and calls for action were gaining ground. The Hampshire Telegraph joined the debate with a graphic account which referred particularly to East Street, Point, and spoke of "an abominable nuisance arising from the stench in that closely-packed and densely populated area." It continued. "The air around the locality to which we advert is impregnated with a foul effluvia, emanating from a stagnant pool at Broad Street side of the Camber, near the old Custom House, where the animal and vegetable manure from the slaughter-houses run and remain, fouling the atmosphere of the whole neighbourhood." The newspaper added that the inhabitatants were "placed in a dangerous condition by the disgusting and nauseous effluvia they are continually breathing." It pointed out that at the Commisariat slaughterhouse in Christmas week alone, 100 head of cattle and between 150 and 200 sheep had been killed.

Vision — Enterprise — Piety

1862

Although not a native of Portsmouth, Thomas Ellis Owen deserves a foremost place in the roll of those men of enterprise and foresight who transformed the city. By profession an architect and civil engineer, he was engaged to carry out a scheme of Camber improvement. Realising the potential value of Portsea Island, he made the place his home and, about 1837, commenced a scheme of building speculation. It was predicted by many that his only prospect was ruin, but they had good reason to change their views as cornfields, meadows, market gardens and marshes were covered with picturesque villas and terraces which attracted residents. He was one of the first advocates of a drainage scheme, and it was due to his enterprise and perseverance that two lines of railways were extended to the town. He became a member of the Corporation in 1831, was chosen as Mayor in 1846, and again in 1862, but a month later he died from heart disease in his 59th year. St Jude's Church was built in 1851 at his own cost, from his own design, and to complete a good story, his daughter married the first Vicar.

The Last of the Stocks

1863

This year the remains of the stocks, used for the punishment of old-time offenders, were removed from the front of the police station in Ordnance Row, Portsea. They were probably broken up for firewood: more's the pity, as they would have made an interesting exhibit in the City Museum. Here, under the date of 1620, is an extract from the Corporation records: "Wee give a paine to ye Chamberlaine of this towne that he doe make up a sufficient paier of Stocks for this Towne for ye punishinge of ofendors betweene this and our Ladye Day next in paine to lose XXs."

In 1733, the Grand Jury made Presentment "against the persons who were concerned in takeing and carrying away the instruments (called the Stocks) within this towne, which were prepared and sett up for the punishment of such offenders who in their nightly revels threw them in the churchyard to be buried among the Monuments of the Dead."

From Circus to Church

1864

It was in this Circus building in Lion Gate Road (now known as Edinburgh Road) that a new church was formed as the result of weekly meetings devoted to religion and the news of the day. The writer, who was a boy of eight at the time, still carried the memory of a great disappointment. Thinking a real circus was in progress, he entered the building and was received as a lamb who had strayed from the fold.

The original Circus, a tent-like building, took its name from the fact that it had previously been used as an equestrian circus. The first service was held there in 1857, and the astonishingly large audience led to a permanent church being built in 1864 in Surrey Street. It was demolished in the late 1950s.

When Milton had a Village Green

1864

At this time Milton was the happy hunting ground of holidaymakers and lovers of the country, for it was a place of real beauty. It was reached through Speck's Lane (now Sandringham Road), which led between hedges of honeysuckle and wild roses to the Village Green, the smithy, and its house of refreshment, well named The Traveller's Joy.

A Moral Plague Spot

1864

Inevitably in a naval port, parts of Victorian Portsmouth earned a notorious reputation, but genteel Southsea did not escape either. The problem is vividly illustrated in the following letter published in the Hampshire Telegraph in March that year, and headed "A Moral Plague Spot." "In our last issue we published a letter, signed 'W.W.,' drawing attention to a monstrous evil which has been permitted to exist for a considerable length of time past without any effectual attempt being made to check it. We refer to the nightly assembly on the main roads crossing Southsea Common of prostitutes of the most vile and abandoned character who, our correspondent said, 'assail every passenger, even in the hearing of the guardian policeman, with their filthy invitations, counched in language the most revolting and obscene.' We are glad to be enabled to state that the forcible appeal of our correspondent has not been without its effect. We understand that the authorities have given instructions to the police to remove these creatures from all places where they are a nuisance to passengers, and more particularly from Southsea Common. The responsibility, therefore, now rests with the police, and there is every reason to belive that this moral plague spot' will soon lose its unenviable reputation."

The Spithead Forts

1864

The defence budget led to as fierce a debate in 1864 as it does in modern times. The bone of contention at that time was the hugely expensive ring of forts which the Government was throwing up around Portsmouth. When Parliament debated the subject at the end of July that year, there were complaints that vital legislation had been pushed through in the early hours of the morning when the few M.P.s in the House were too fatigued to pay proper attention. One Member made a particularly spirited attack during the third reading of the Fortifications (Provision for Expenses) Bill, and poured his heaviest ammunition against the four Spithead forts. Complaining that the nation seemed to be "in a sort of fool's paradise," he asserted that although we had "an enormous line of entrenchments and casements, we had neither soldiers to man them nor guns to put into them." At sea, we had not a single floating battery. The country had ironclad ships of great efficiency, but no suitable guns for them. The Ordnance Committee had reported that the new 100-pounder was of little use, and the only gun the country had to rely on was the old 68-pounder smooth bore. There was an immediate rebuttal from the Marquis of Hartington, who reminded the House that the plan was to defend Spithead with a system of forts in combination with floating defences, so that if an enemy ship managed to penetrate the outer line of defence, it would be exposed to fire from the forts. None was more than 3,000 yards from its neighbour, and experiments had shown that a 600-pounder gun could penetrate an ironclad at that distance. Any enemy ship must come within 1,500 yards of a fort, and even it it reached a position where it could shell the dockyard, would be exposed to the combined fire of all four forts. The Marquis admitted that the country was not as advanced in ordnance as he would have liked, but assured doubting Members that by the time the forts were complete the following summer, the armament for them would be ready. The Bill — and the huge expense involved — was duly passed.

Visit of the French Fleet

1865

This year witnessed the beginning of the Entente Cordiale with France, when her fleet of nine ironclads and other vessels came to Spithead. The superiority of her ships gave us a shock and taught us a lesson. In addition to naval receptions, the Municipality under the leadership of the Mayor, Richard William Ford, gave generous entertainment, the town was gaily decorated, and all went merrily as a wedding bell. Even the little naval orphans, of which the writer was one, were taken for a cruise around the combined fleets.

The Mayor, by the way, was one of the ablest and most progressive the city has ever known. He was a strong advocate of arterial drainage, which he had the satisfaction of inaugurating this year. He was also an earnest advocate of municipal enterprise, and had his short-sighted colleagues taken his advice, they could have bought the entire water supply system for £42,000. Now in private hands, it is worth millions. To complete the record of his noble life, he established the Eye and Ear Hospital in 1884.

The situation at this time was not quite as gloomy as W.G. Gates made out. It is true that France had established naval supremacy for a short time, but Britain's ironclad Navy — which started in 1860 with H.M.S. Warrior — had grown rapidly by the time of the French Fleet's visit.

Croxton Town

1865

That part of Southsea now covered by the Terraces was formerly known as Croxton Town by way of compliment to its owner. In 1711, the entire site had been sold for only £100, but when it was sold off in plots in the early 19th Century, it fetched £17,000. A house in the roadway was occupied by Thomas Croxton and was not removed until the first tramway to Southsea Pier was laid down in 1864.

Far less is known of this early property speculator than his more celebrated counterpart, Thomas Owen, who developed much of the nearby land at about the same time. Croxton was buried in St Thomas's churchyard.

On the Road to Portsea

1865

In the days of the old fortifications, Prospect Road was a thoroughfare not more than twelve feet wide, with a high rampart on one side and several public houses on the other. It was regarded as a very evil resort and shunned by decent people after dark. At the northern end it was possible to pass through the rampart and cross the moat by a small bridge to the road leading to Portsea by the King's Mill, the Mill Gate and Mill Pond.

Election by Open Vote

1865

There were many stirring scenes in St George's Square, Portsea, when one of the last Parliamentary elections by open voting resulted in the return of Serjeant Gaselee, the Liberal candidate. The hustings had been erected by the east wall of St George's Church, and as the compiler of these records had been given a holiday from school, he is even now, 80 years later, able to recall the "jolly good time" he and his companions had that day.

Serjeant Gaselee's grandfather was an eminent surgeon. He served as an alderman of the borough and as Mayor in 1797 and 1802. The family were generous supporters of local institutions, and the Judge took such interest in the Beneficial Society in Portsea that his son, the Serjeant, presented a very fine portrait. It is on record that Charles Dickens was much distressed when told of the anger of the Gaselee family because of the caricature of the Judge as "Justice Stareleigh" in the trial in Pickwick Papers.

A Serjeant at this time was a barrister of the highest rank. Stephen Gaselee was one of two Liberals elected. It is interesting to note that even after the Reform Bill, the total number of votes cast at this election was less than 8,000.

Story of the Portsmouth Trams

1865

In May of this year the first street tramway was opened in Portsmouth. It conveyed passengers and luggage from the railway station at Landport to Clarence Pier. The Manager, Mr. A.W. White, a most enterprising and far-seeing man, continued to develop the system until the whole town was admirably served. Generous and kind-hearted, he was much admired by the public, who presented him with a handsome testimonial, but he only received grudging help from the Corporation. In 1901 the Corporation exercised its power under the Tramways Act of 1870 by taking over the undertaking at its material value, without compensation, but the smile on the face of the Council changed to gloom when Mr. White informed them that the first section from the railway station was authorised and constructed as a street railway which was not affected by the Tramways Act, and for this portion the Council had to pay a handsome sum as compensation.

These horse-drawn trams had a somewhat cautious start, and the new carriages were twice thrown off the rails during experimental runs to accustom the animals to their new work.

The Last Visit of Charles Dickens

1866

In May, Charles Dickens gave readings from his famous works in the city of his birth. They were heard by hundreds in St George's Hall, Portsea, and there were few dry eyes when he uttered the prayer of Tiny Tim: "God bless us, every one."

The celebrated author was said to have "riveted his audience" for two hours on two evenings, and the Hampshire Telegraph commented: "He can touch every chord of human sympathy with an intensity of power which would be almost painful if it were long sustained."

An Expanding Dockyard

1867

A great extension of the Dockyard was started this year, the estimated cost being £1,500,000. It was proposed to extend the area of the Yard to 300 acres, to add seven docks, some with a depth of 40 feet, to treble the number of basins and extend six fold their size.

The land for this ambitious scheme was obtained by demolishing the old fortifications, including the celebrated ramparts, and reclaiming more than 90 acres of mud — a skill at which Portsmouth was to become increasingly adept in subsequent years.

"Form, Riflemen, Form!"

1868

Due in large measure to the efforts of the Government to prepare the nation to resist an expected invasion, and to a stirring appeal by the Poet Laureate (Lord Tennyson), the Volunteer movement spread rapidly. Portsmouth and Gosport soon had a fine body of amateur soldiers. This year, Colonel Edwin Galt, the Mayor, succeeded in arranging a great Volunteer Review at Easter, in which some 28,000 men from this district and South Hampshire took part, to the joyous satisfaction of the populace. There was a sham fight on Portsdown and a review on Southsea Common.

Galt was Colonel of the 2nd Hampshire Volunteer Artillery, which had been formed in 1860, but there was also a number of rifle corps in the surrounding area and a Boat Brigade. Fierce rivalries developed, particularly when former regular officers discovered that an enthusiastic amateur in a neighbouring corps outranked them.

"This is the Blue Postesses" and an Ancient Coaching House

1870

The Blue Posts, which was destroyed by fire in May, was one of the oldest inns in the town, having been built as far back as 1613. It was also one of the principal coaching houses in the borough before the railway era. It was much frequented by the younger officers of the Navy, and is thus referred to by Marryat in one of his famous stories:

"This is the Blue Postesses,
Where Midshipmen leave their chestesses,
Call for tea and toastesses,
And forget to pay for their breakfastesses."

"A noted spot was Point," wrote the author of *Jem Bunt*. "There stood the inviting Blue Posts, where many a hungry reefer has enjoyed his tea for two and toast for six. Oh, it was a delectable sight to witness the eagerness with which the young gentlemen regaled themselves, damning the waiters to show that they were real officers and topping the grandee in extraordinary style, without the least fear of being brought up all standing by the first lieutenant. There also stood the Star and Garter, but that was more of a lieutenant's house — a touch of the higher grade — a sort of weather-side entertainment for man and horse. I frequented it in later days when I crept from under the lee of the mizzen-staysail, but though refreshments were excellent and the company somewhat silent, yet I never felt so much at ease or revelled in such unbounded luxury as at the dear old Blue Posts."

Although fortunately no one was injured, the blaze spread rapidly through the old building and defied the efforts of the Landport fire engine, plus firemen from the Royal Artillery and Clarence Barracks, to contain it. The original inn took its name from the bright blue pillars which stood at the entrance to the stable yard and the bar.

Where Landport had its Beginning

1870

This picture of the junction of Commercial Road and Lion Gate Road (as it was known at this time) is of more than passing interest. The Bedford Hotel, which we are told was patronised by His Royal Highness the Prince of Wales, stood on the site of the first house of refreshment in this district. It was known as the Halfway House as it was about midway between Portsea and Kingston Church. The sketch also shows the newly-erected memorial to Admiral Sir Charles Napier, which was later removed to Victoria Park.

A Tragedy of the Night

1870

On August 4th, 1870, the Captain, a twin-screw iron-clad constructed on Captain Cowper Coles' plan, left Portsmouth on an experimental cruise with a portion of the Channel Fleet. She had given rise to a good deal of discussion because of her massive top hamper and low freeboard, which sailors said made her liable to turn over. During the night of September 6th, when the Fleet was in the Bay of Biscay, the wind freshened, and when morning dawned there was a significant blank in the squadron. Of the 11 ships which sailed into the night, only ten sailed into the morning. A ghastly catastrophe had occurred, the Captain had overturned, and out of a crew of nearly 500 souls, only 18 were saved, the rest, including Captain Coles, perishing mid the unbroken darkness of the night. A sum of £58,000 was publicly subscribed for the benefit of the widows and orphans.

This disaster hit Portsmouth particularly hard. The 18 survivors said the ship went bottom up in a heavy squall and sank in three minutes. The Hampshire Telegraph reported: "Scores of houses in the town were plunged into the deepest distress; in every direction there was but one topic of discussion; and never do we remember an event to have filled the town with a greater degree of horror." The Captain had been regarded as a crack vessel, and the ship of the future. Among the victims was the Hon. Arthur Baring, a 16-year-old naval cadet and the grandson of the late Sir Francis Baring, who had been a Portsmouth M.P. for 39 years.

The Navy Abolishes Flogging

1871

The days of the lash were numbered as a result of a decision taken by the Admiralty that year to abolish flogging for all but the most severe offences. The House of Commons was told that in future, imprisonment would be the norm wherever possible, except for cases of mutiny, violence to a superior officer, aggravated desertion, or "offences which, from contagion, might endanger the safety of a ship." The Hampshire Telegraph commented: "There are scores of men, we presume, in Portsmouth who remember when 'four dozen' was the penalty for the most trivial offences, or perhaps for no offences at all." It added: "To a Liberal Government we are indebted for the all but total abolition of a punishment which ought never to be inflicted except under special circumstances." Flogging had already been abolished in the Army, except in time of war, on the line of march, or when troops were embarked on board ship.

The Fountain

1872

This inn in the High Street, which claimed a life of at least 300 years, had been a coaching house and the favourite resort of naval lieutenants. It was said to be haunted, and what stories the ghosts could tell! It was also noted for a "punch" which was guaranteed to intoxicate anyone who partook of it. The inn contained many secret hiding places which were used when the Press Gangs were ashore.

One visitor, describing her first inspection, wrote: "We admired the wide old staircase and the dark wood panelling of the first floor, but it was dreadful higher up. You stumbled up and down into rooms with a treacherous step in the doorway. There were secret stairs in the thickness of the wall all the way up from the bar, and openings on every floor contrived for men's escape from the Press Gangs."

At the height of its fame, the Fountain was said to be capable of accommodating 170 people as guests, and 200 in the dining room. It was also the starting point of one of the many stage coaches in earlier days. In 1874 it was bought by Miss Sarah Robinson and converted into a home for soldiers. The building was one of the many destroyed during the Second World War.

A Portsmouth Martyr

1873

Dr. George Turner, a man of Portsmouth, was this year appointed its first Medical Officer of Health. After many years of useful service in this country and South Africa, he devoted himself to research for a remedy for the terrible scourge of leprosy, and in this work he also contracted the disease. Hearing of his self-sacrifice, King Edward VII conferred upon him the honour of knighthood. In a letter to the Corporation of Portsmouth, Sir George wrote: "Very few of those I remember are left, and I hear the angels calling me sometimes. What troubles me is that I have no voice and no ear for music, and what I shall do with that harp I cannot conceive." On March 15th, 1915, he joined the angels.

The Cost of Crime

1874

Because the site of the jail in Penny Street was required by the War Office for barracks extension, the Corporation were constrained to build a new jail at Milton for a cost of £35,611. Soon after completion, the Government took it over, and the ratepayers had to pay the debt in full. The writer had the doubtful privilege of being the first to be confined for a brief space in one of the cells, just to see what it was like.

Five Post Lane

1874

Alfred Road, leading from Lion Gate Road (now Edinburgh Road) to Unicorn Road, was opened this year. It took the place of an ancient pathway through the fortifications and was known as Five Post Lane. For many years the entrance was the scene daily of great activity, and you could buy from itinerant vendors anything from boiled whelks to certain cures for all the ills of human life. It was opposite this lane, in 1842, that the Keys of the Garrison were first presented to Queen Victoria, who admired them so much that, contrary to all precedent, she retained them for an hour or more when she went into the Dockyard.

The Convicts' Good Record

1876

During the work of enlarging the Dockyard, full use was made of the services of the convicts, several hundred in number. To maintain guard over them, a number of observation towers were built upon the outer wall, but as the men were very well treated there were very few attempts at escape. Some of the towers can be seen today in Gunwharf Road as part of the perimeter wall of H.M.S. Vernon.

The Great Mill Pond is Blotted Out

1876

For several centuries after Portsmouth had acquired importance, an arm of the sea entered from the harbour, where Vernon now is, and helped to extend considerably the area covered by what became known as the Mill Pond. It was, in fact, known as the Great Lake in the earliest years of its existence, as it was fed not only from the tides from the harbour but by a considerable stream of fresh water which ran from what was then known as Lake Gate, across the main road to Portsea, where it discharged into the Great Lake, or Maudlin Pond as it was also named. From time to time as the town developed, portions were filled in by the engineers, and by 1876 it was improved out of existence, the only link with the far past being an inlet from the harbour to the Vernon establishment. At the end of the 19th Century, the Corps of Royal Engineers established its official quarters on a portion of the reclaimed land.

The Birth of a Great Adventure

1877

Mr. James Graham Niven deserves a place in the story as the founder of the Evening News. For some time (as the writer, who joined the staff in July, 1877, can testify), it seemed that the venture would fail, but eventually the very small evening sheet became a public necessity. The office was in Arundel Street and Mr. Niven drove a dog cart to take the paper to various parts of the town.

The paper was born in a disused butcher's shop in April, 1877. Consisting of four broadsheet pages, it sold at a halfpenny. Type was hand set by six compositors in a cramped upper bedroom, and the press was installed in a former slaughterhouse at the rear of the building. At the outset, Niven was manager, editor, reporter and distributor, but within a few months the paper's circulation had doubled — to 4,000 copies — and he took on a young reporter named William Gates. In 1895, the paper moved to purpose-built premises in Stanhope Road, where it stayed until 1969. The move to an imaginative new building at Hilsea was accompanied by a change of name to The News. Today, the paper employs more than 600 people based at The News Centre and at branch offices throughout Hampshire and West Sussex.

Tantivy! Tantivy!

1877

Andrew Nance, who died in December this year, was a man of mark. He was born at the Fountain Hotel, which, with the Blue Posts and the Crown Inn, were kept by his father, one of the principal posting masters. His son, Andrew, for a time drove the famous Tantivy coach between Portsmouth and London, and on one occasion did the journey in five hours 42 minutes. He was elected a councillor for All Saints ward, but was deposed by the burgesses because he dared advocate the introduction of the railway to Portsmouth. He was re-elected for St Paul's ward, and in 1854 served the office of Mayor.

"Both Land and Sea Ring with Thy Name, Eurydice"

1878

In May, 1843, the Eurydice, of 26 guns, was launched at Portsmouth, and a local poet thus concluded his paean of praise:

"Hail to thee, modern beauty, hail,
Success and honour with thee sail,
Till, as of old, both land and sea
Ring with thy name, Eurydice."

Alas, the day did come when land and sea did ring with her name, and there was deep sorrow in the sound. On the afternoon of Sunday, March 24th, 1878, the Eurydice, then a training ship, was off Ventnor, Isle of Wight, homeward bound with all sail set, when she was struck by a sudden and most violent gale of wind and snow, and sank with all hands save two.

In connection with this sad loss, a remarkable story of second sight was told by Dr. Boyd Carpenter, a former Bishop of Ripon. He was in the room of Sir John Cowell at Windsor, in company with that gentleman and Sir John MacNeill, when the latter suddenly exclaimed: "Good heavens, why don't they close the portholes and reef the topsails?" Sir John Cowell asked what he meant and he replied that he hardly knew, but he had seen a ship coming up Channel in full sail with open portholes, while a heavy squall was descending upon her. At the very time of his conversation, the fatal storm fell upon Eurydice.

This wooden sailing frigate, built to traditional design, was said to have "admirable sea-going qualities." Her crew was composed almost entirely of young unmarried ratings on a training cruise. Five men were pulled from the sea by a schooner, but one was already dead and two more died on the way to Ventnor. The sole survivors of a crew of more than 300 were an able seaman and a first class boy. The story concerning the Bishop's friend and his second sight would have appealed to W.G. Gates, a lifelong spiritualist and a firm believer in unearthly messages.

Trouble Ahead

1878

Nineteenth century fashion posed a particular problem for some of the town's gentlemen as they went about their business. The trouble lay in the universal practice of wearing hats, and was exemplified by one man whose complaint about "tradesmen's nuisances" reached the letters column of the Hampshire Telegraph in April that year:

"Sir — I really feel obliged to endorse "G.L.W.'s" letter of the 26th ultimo concerning tradesmen's nuisances, for the awnings, &c., are really disgraceful. It was only on Saturday last that going up Middle-street, the awning of the draper at the corner (Mr. Coombes I believe it is) knocked my hat off in the mud, which is not very pleasant in the rain. This awning is only about 4ft. 9in. high over the kerb, and it is time some one took measures to compel this, and others, to be heightened. I am not overgrown, I may add, as some correspondent hinted concerning G.L.W., nor am I an habitual grumbler.

I remain, Yours obediently,'
ANTE-NUISANCE'
Southsea, April 8

Southsea Enjoys the Fruits of Peace

1879

Southseas place as a fashionable resort was firmly established this year with the opening of yet another pier, this time at South Parade. The ceremony was performed by Princess Edward of Saxe-Weimar, to whom the pier's engineer, Mr. George Rake, explained that although earlier plans had fallen through, "Southsea had become a great and fashionable watering place" and the time for another promenade over the sea had arrived. Pile-driving operations had been made difficult for about a tenth of the pier's 600-foot length because of the remains of a submerged forest or belt of trees. The structure took six months to build and cost just over £9,000.

South Parade Pier's history is not short of drama. Badly damaged by fire in 1904, it was left derelict for two years before the decision to rebuild was taken. Between the two world wars, it became a lively entertainment centre with a splendid concert pavilion, and it was near the pier in 1944 that special landing stages were constructed for thousands of troops to embark for the D-Day invasion of Northern France. In 1974, another serious fire broke out during the filming of a rock musical and seemed to have threatened South Parade's future, but it survived for yet another rebuilding.

The Victoria Barracks

1880

Victoria Barracks were built this year on a portion of the glacis which formerly curtained Old Portsmouth. Much of the work was done by convicts, who were marched under guard from the prison at Portsea near the Anchor Gate. Public pity was shown by the dropping of little packets of tobacco and sweets as the men passed. One of the convicts who carved the heraldic devices on the apex of the main building is said to have asked to be kept on after his sentence had expired so that he might finish the work.

These magnificently flamboyant barracks eventually passed to the Navy in 1945 and were used for ten years to house new entrants. There was then a plan for them to become the home of the Royal Hampshire Regiment, but this did not come about and argument over their future continued for some years. When demolition started in 1967, workmen uncovered a thick wall several feet below the surface, believed to be part of the old defences in the moat. The site is now occupied by the Crest Hotel and the Pembroke Park housing development.

The Greatest Snowstorm on Record. Traffic Suspended and Prices Rise

1881

On January 18th, Portsmouth and Gosport were visited by a snowstorm of unparalleled severity. It fell to the depth of several feet, all traffic was suspended, the prices of necessities rose rapidly, a public relief fund was opened, and nearly a fortnight elapsed before the streets were clear. Portsmouth Corporation spent £1,100 in a partial clearing.

The ferocity of the blizzard can be imagined by the fact that Stubbington Lane, North End, was reported to have been under seven feet of snow, while Port Creek and Fareham Creek froze over. Business in both towns was almost totally suspended, the tramways stopped, and all sailings between the Isle of Wight and the mainland were cancelled. A train which left Portsmouth Town station at 11.25 a.m. on January 18th ran into a snowdrift at Port Creek and became hopelessly stuck, with the snow piling up so rapidly that none of the carriage doors could be opened. Three engines were sent to try to free the train, but with no effect, and the unfortunate passengers were trapped until 8 p.m., when an army of workmen eventually succeeded in shovelling their way through the snow so that planks could be laid to the windows.

Beauty in Religion

1881

It was in July of this year that the handsome Baptist Church in Elm Grove, Southsea, was opened, and it contributed much to the religious life of the city. But it was entirely destroyed in 1941 by the Germans while engaged on their devilish work of destruction. The house next to it was occupied by Dr. Arthur Conan Doyle when he started his famous career as historian and novelist.

The first Baptists had made their appearance in Portsmouth in 1704, when a group from Gosport founded a society and built a chapel in what came to be known as Meeting House Alley. Subsequent chapels were erected in White's Row, Clarence Street, Great Southsea Street, and Lake Lane.

The Sailors' Angel

1882

This year Agnes Weston, as the sailors lovingly called her, opened the first portion of the Sailors' Rest in Commercial Road, and with most extensive additions it proved for many years a haven of rest and refreshment. She had a most devoted assistant in Miss Sophie Wintz, and together they ministered not only to the comfort and well-being of thousands of sailors who made it their home, but they also took the men's wives and sweethearts under their wing, a service which they acknowledged by the presentation of a portrait to the city. When Miss Weston died in 1918, the Admiralty accorded her the unprecedented honour of a naval funeral. Unhappily, the buildings raised with so much loving care were destroyed by the Germans in 1941.

A similar Rest was opened in Devonport, and both familiarly became known as "Aggie Weston's." Miss Wintz was made a Dame in 1921, and she, too, was given a naval funeral when she died eight years later.

The Changing of the Guard

1883

Another link with a picturesque past was broken this year by the removal of the main Guard Room from Grand Parade. For many years it had been the magnet which attracted a crowd of people every night to witness the Changing of the Guard, to discuss the news of the day, to watch with envy or amusement the courting couples, and then to march in step with the band as it passed through the High Street to the Barracks. On special occasions, spectators were treated to a musical programme outside Government House. A cross was erected there by the Second Battalion of the King's Regiment to their comrades who fell in the Indian Mutiny. It was afterwards removed to Liverpool when that town was chosen as the Territorial home of the Battalion.

The Catholic Cathedral

1887

In July of this year the Roman Catholic See of Portsmouth was created, the first Bishop being Monsignor Vertue. The Cathedral in Edinburgh Road was opened with impressive ceremony, naval and military officers in full dress uniform carrying the canopy over the new Bishop. Only a small part of the Cathedral was completed in time for the opening, and it was eventually finished in 1892. Before this time, Portsmouth had been part of the enormous Diocese of Southwark, which covered all counties south of the Thames, as well as the Channel Islands.

St Mary's, Portsea

1887

The third Church of St Mary, opened this year, was the result of a splendid endeavour by the Rev. Edgar Jacob and the munificence of Mr. W.H. Smith, First Lord of the Admiralty. It is worthy of note that Canon Jacob became Bishop of Newcastle, that his successor, the Rev. Cosmo Gordon Lang, became Archbishop of Canterbury, and that his successor at Portsmouth, the Rev. Cyril Garbett, became Archbishop of York.

Because of its links with these celebrated clerics, St Mary's became known as "the nest of Bishops." When Edgar Jacob took over as Vicar, the church was at a low ebb, but he was responsible for a phenomenal growth in both congregation and activity. His acquaintance with W.H. Smith, Cabinet Minister and son of the founder of the celebrated bookseller's, was more than fortunate, as Smith provided more than half the cost of the new church.

A Maker of Modern Portsmouth

1888

Among the makers of modern Portsmouth, a foremost place must be given to Alderman Emanuel Emanuel, who died this year. Entering the Town Council in 1844, he declined to take the oath on "the faith of a Christian" and thereby rendered himself liable to a fine of £500 for every vote he gave, but there was no one in Portsmouth mean enough to proceed against this valiant Jew. He was a reformer to his fingertips. Free Mart Fair having become a great nuisance, he campaigned for its abolition. As Southsea Common was a waste, polluted by open drains and occasionally swept by the sea, he secured the favour of the Governor, Lord Frederick Fitzclarence, in the construction of the Esplanade and the levelling of the Common. He also helped in securing the People's Park (as Victoria Park was first named), in promoting the railway to London, and in many other ways worked as a brave and true pioneer.

A High Street jeweller, Alderman Emanuel became known for his charity and hospitality, and one of the highlights of his year as Mayor in 1866 was the visit of the Sultan of Turkey. A drinking fountain to his memory can be seen at Canoe Lake, Southsea.

The Town Hall

1890

The new Town Hall, which had been built at a cost of £137,098, was opened with fitting ceremony on August 9th by the Prince and Princess of Wales. "You have," said the Prince, "every reason to feel proud of this fine building, worthy of the largest naval port in the United Kingdom, and of the architectural beauties which it displays." But the pride of the inhabitants turned to fury when, on the night of January 10th, 1941, the whole of the interior with its precious contents was destroyed by fire from bombs rained upon the city by the Germans. Happily, the tower stood firm and thus was saved from destruction the ancient records of the Corporation and the priceless collection of silver plate.

The Last of the Military Governors

1890

The Duke of Connaught, a son of Queen Victoria, was appointed as Military Commander of the Garrison of Portsmouth, the last of a long line of officers who had held the position. The list goes back to the year 1290, the office in those days combining the Governorship of Portchester as well as Portsmouth. As the last of the Governors, it does not seem without significance that the Duke should also occupy the last Government House, which had been built on a portion of the ancient Glacis and which was destroyed by the Germans when they blasted the city in 1941.

A Double Christening

1891

There were many occasions on which Queen Victoria honoured Portsmouth. She reviewed the Fleet in 1842, attended the first Regatta after the opening of Clarence Esplanade, gave generous support to the Royal Sailors' Home, and inspected several hundred wounded men home from the Crimea. She presented the first Victoria Crosses on Southsea Common, and on February 26th, 1891, she was made happy by a great public demonstration when she christened two new warships, the Royal Sovereign and Royal Arthur. To mark the occasion, she conferred a knighthood upon the Mayor, William Pink. Portsmouth remembered with pride that it was a Royal Sovereign that was the first warship to be dry-docked here in 1496, thus creating a world's record.

Light on the Path

1892

To Sir Thomas Scott Foster the citizens of Portsmouth owe their possession of the electric supply system. During his Mayoralty this year, the Town Council was asked to decide whether an electricity system should be introduced and controlled by a private company or by the Corporation. When a vote was taken, there was an equal division so the Mayor was asked to give a casting vote and, as a true and wise citizen, he voted in favour of the Corporation.

Sir Thomas also tried to secure public ownership of the town's water supply, but on this occasion vested interests proved too powerful.

An Icy Start

1894

The first week of the year was a bitterly cold one, with the thermometer at the Dockyard gates falling to 14 degrees and country roads around Portsmouth under several inches of snow. Both moats at Hilsea were covered in ice, Fareham Creek partly froze over, and skaters were out at Brockhurst moats at Gosport. The horse tram service had to be suspended as the animals could not keep their feet on the icy roads.

Another Link Broken

1894

Another link with the past was broken by the demolition of the Van Office at Point. This was mainly used for goods traffic to and from London, but a few passengers were also carried, though not in comfort, at half the price of a seat in one of the stage coaches. This cheaper and bumpy ride was mainly chosen by sailors.

"Heaven's Light Our Guide"

1894

The last of the Indian troopships left Portsmouth, to the profound regret of all the inhabitants. The passage of these beautiful vessels, so graceful in their lines, so conspicuous in their white dress with the broad band of distinctive colour, was one of the delights of residents and visitors. They each bore the motto of the Star of India, which Portsmouth has chosen for its own — "Heaven's Light Our Guide."

Looking for Work

1894

A deputation of working men visited Portsea Island Board of Guardians at the beginning of this year to urge some sort of help for the unemployed. Their spokesman, Mr. Slingsby Godfrey, secretary of Portsmouth branch of the Fabian Society, handed in a list of 310 names of men who were willing to work but could not find a job. After a special meeting, the Guardians decided that each man should be given a ticket and told to attend each day at the Corporation yard in Anglesea Road between 6 and 7 a.m., to wait for work. Preference would be given to married men with children.

Father Dolling's Sacrifice

1895

Portsmouth lost one of its most devoted and popular ministers when Father Robert Dolling sacrificed his position rather than his faith. The beautiful church of St Agatha was built by his endeavours in one of the poorest quarters of the city, but when completed, the Bishop refused to consecrate it unless an altar to the Living Dead was removed. To the sorrow of countless admirers, Father Dolling was thus driven from the district which he had done so much to serve, and the people he had devoted his life to save.

A tireless worker for the city's poor and destitute, Dolling threw open his house to all comers and campaigned hard and long against social ills. When he came to St Agatha's there were a mere handful of communicants: when he left after ten years, the figure was more than 400. The Church, however, could not tolerate his practice of saying masses for the dead. He died, aged 51, in 1902. Dolling's book, "Ten Years in a Portsmouth Slum," is an absorbing account both of his ministry in the city and of the difficulties which led to his leaving. St Agatha's ceased to be a place of worship in 1954 and then spent some years as a naval storehouse. After several plans to demolish the building, it was listed as a place of architectural and historic interest, and in 1987 a restoration appeal was launched to preserve it as a museum.

A Dream That Came True

1895

On the first day of the year, the parish of St Matthew at Southsea came into being. In the years that followed, one of the finest churches in this city, or any other, was built and paid for, thanks to the spiritual enthusiasm and the engaging personality of its Vicar, the Rev. E. Bruce Cornford. Had he been on this side of life when the Huns came in 1941 and blasted his beloved Church to ruins, it would have broken his heart.

This rapidly expanding area had doubled its population in just over ten years as more and more rows of late Victorian houses sprang up, and the temporary church at the corner of Heyward Road and Fawcett Road was soon outgrown. The enthusiastic Bruce Cornford went on to strike a controversial note when he refused to celebrate the official day of thanksgiving which followed the end of the Boer War. He told parishioners he could not thank God for our success in taking hold of a country which did not belong to us.

Forty Years in Parliament

1901

This year the finest Drill Hall in the South of England was opened by the Earl of Northbrook, whose father, Sir Francis Thornhill Baring, represented Portsmouth in Parliament for 40 years. In 1866 he was raised to the peerage as Baron Northbrook, and the Corporation rightly interpreted public sentiment when it placed on record its "satisfaction and appreciation of his past services, and its thanks for the faithful, honourable and independent manner in which he discharged his duties during the 40 years he represented the borough in Parliament." To the general regret, he did not live long to enjoy the honour conferred upon him, as he died on September 6th. During the First World War, the Drill Hall suffered such damage that its noble tower had to be demolished.

Sir Francis Baring first entered Parliament in 1826, and was a staunch supporter of the Reform Bill of 1832 which extended the voting franchise. He later became Chancellor of the Exchequer and then First Lord of the Admiralty.

A Great Queen Passes

1901

On the first day of February, Portsmouth sorrowfully witnessed the passing of a great Queen. Through a long line of British and foreign warships, with flags at half mast and firing minute guns, the body of Victoria was borne across the Solent she knew so well. As the Royal Yacht entered the harbour, the last gleams of the winter sun shone forth. The sky for a few moments glowed red, and then grey mists veiled the ships. The Navy had said farewell. As Princess Victoria, the Queen made her first acquaintance with Portsmouth from the windows of the George Hotel, where she had been taken to see the room which Nelson had last occupied. On the day of her Coronation, the Portsmouth public purchased a beautiful portrait of the young Queen, but alas, it perished with other treasures when the Germans fired the city in 1941.

The General's Dream Comes True

1901

This year the Freedom of Portsmouth was conferred on General Sir Frederick FitzWygram in recognition of his kindness in allowing his beautiful estate at Leigh Park to be used as a holiday resort for the inhabitants, and especially the children. He was a man of wide sympathies and generous deeds. The writer, who is a bit of a visionary, is quite sure that the spirit of Sir Frederick experienced a thrill of joyous satisfaction when he realised the estate had been secured in perpetuity for the citizens of Portsmouth through the clever advocacy of Councillor F.G.H. Storey.

The phrasing used here by W.G. Gates reveals his lifelong interest in spiritualism. Members of his family recall the seances he used to attend, and his deep-seated conviction that there could be communication with "the other side of life." The part played by Councillor Frederick Storey in the purchase of Leigh Park is told elsewhere.

To the Immortal Memory

1903

This year the Corporation wisely purchased the house in Commercial Road in which Charles Dickens was born, and converted it into a museum for the exhibition of relics and pictures of Portsmouth's immortal townsman.

A Salute from the Sailors of the U.S.A.

1903

Due to the loyal inspiration of the Mayor, Colonel Sir William Dupree, a statue of Queen Victoria in Town Hall Square was unveiled with befitting ceremony on July 7th. By happy coincidence, a squadron of American warships had arrived at Spithead and a number of officers and men from it lined up around the memorial and saluted as it was unveiled and the National Anthem was played.

By the death of Sir William in 1930, Portsmouth lost a citizen whose life had been intimately associated with varied phases of public welfare as magistrate, councillor, alderman, mayor, and Colonel of Volunteers. To close a fine career he gave a large sum of money to place on a sound financial basis the Industrial League, the object being to improve relations between employer and employed. For this wise and generous act, he was honoured with a Baronetcy.

The Stars and Stripes flew at Southsea Pier to welcome the battleship Kearsage, the cruisers Chicago and San Francisco, and the gunboat Machias. Newspaper coverage of the visit made envious comparisons between the U.S. sailor's lavish diet and choice of menu, and the Royal Navy's hard tack. One American officer remarked: "I never knew a man yet who was able to get through all the rations he is allowed."

Home from the Sea

1903

In September, a Naval Barracks was opened for the men who had been quartered in hulks in the harbour. The building occupied the site of Anglesea Barracks, a public thoroughfare known as Annesley Road, and a portion of the glacis and filled-in moats of the old fortifications. It accommodated 4,000 men and covered an area of nearly 100 acres.

Poor Old Pompey

1904

The question is often asked: "Why is Portsmouth referred to as Pompey?" Many people were under the impression that a warship of that name was either built or associated with the town, but this is not the case. There was a French 74-gun ship of that name captured at Toulon in 1793, and also an earlier Pompey, a small warship engaged in the bombardment of Cartagena in 1740, but in neither of these cases was there are any close association with Portsmouth.

In one of her many addresses to sailors, Miss Agnes Weston, the founder of the Sailors' Rest, told the story of Pompey the Great, and when she described with virtuous anger how, after the Battle of Pharsalia, he was treacherously murdered, one of her audience, moved to compassion, cried out "Poor old Pompey." Others in the audience repeated the words. A few days later, many of these men were at a football match at Fratton Park when the goalkeeper fell in a brave effort to stop the ball. Thereupon one of the sailors cried out "Poor old Pompey!" Others took up the cry, and thus it came about that Portsmouth is now known in the Navy and beyond as Pompey.

Gates's explanation has an intriguing ring about it, but as there are almost as many explanations for the name as there are Portmuthians, the argument will no doubt continue.

Tragedy of the Antarctic

1904

The Antarctic exploration ship Discovery being at Portsmouth, the Mayor, Major John Edward Pink, entertained the officers and crew at a banquet in the Guildhall. Congratulations were showered upon the gallant explorers, there being then no shadow of the calamity which later overtook Captain Scott and his companions, providing a most poignantly tragic scene in the history of Polar exploration. A memorial to the Captain was placed in Portsmouth Dockyard.

The life-size bronze statue of the legendary Scott of the Antarctic was designed by his widow and unveiled on February 24th, 1915. It originally stood on the Parade, but was moved in 1949 to its present position outside the office of the Admiral Superintendent.

Portsea Island under one Government

1905

After a Corporate existence of 800 years, Parliamentary sanction was obtained for an extension of the boundaries to include the whole of Portsea Island. In 1920, the boundaries were further extended to include the whole of the parish of Wymering on the west, to a point beyond Christ Church in the north, and to Drayton in the east.

Battleship Revolution

1906

All records were broken in the construction of the battleship Dreadnought. Laid down in Portsmouth Dockyard on October 2nd, 1905, the vessel was on the stocks less than five months, being christened by King Edward VII on February 12th, 1906. Portsmouth deserves the more credit from the fact that she was designed by Sir Philip Watts, the son of a Dockyard timber inspector. Sir Philip entered the Dockyard as a shipwright apprentice in 1861. In due course he won a scholarship at South Kensington, next was appointed Assistant Constructor at the Admiralty, and was finally entrusted with the revolutionary project of designing the Dreadnought.

Thousands watched the launch of the great vessel, "looking very trim and neat in her coat of grey and red paint." The King walked to the launching platform between a guard of honour of 100 seamen from the Royal Naval Barracks and 100 members of the Royal Marine Light Infantry from Forton. Just as the workmen began to knock away the last blocks to let Dreadnought slide into the water, they sang the "Pompey Chimes," much to the King's amusement.

A Present from Pittsburg

1906

Councillor William T. Dittman, a pioneer in municipal reform, obtained a grant from Andrew Carnegie, the Pittsburg millionaire, for the provision of a new public library at Kingston. It proved to be quite a model of its kind. The councillor was also the main instrument in securing a municipal telephone exchange, which proved quite a success but eventually had to be merged with the national system.

A Pioneer in Good Works

1906

Among the makers of modern Portsmouth, a foremost place must be given to Sir William Pink. He was five times Mayor of the borough. As a mark of Royal appreciation, he received the honour of knighthood, and four years later the Freedom of the Borough was bestowed upon him. In 1891 he had the honour of welcoming the officers and men of the French Fleet, and so handsomely were they entertained that the President of the French Republic conferred upon him the distinction of a Knight of the Legion of Honour. One of his happiest successes was the provision of public libraries, but the greatest pleasure of his public life, as he declared to the compiler of this panorama, was the gift of a handsome clock from the working classes of the borough, paid for by a subscription of a penny, no one being allowed to give more.

The Mayor's High Purpose

1908

The Mayor, Alderman F.G. Foster, who had for 13 years zealously promoted the cause of higher education, had the supreme satisfaction of opening the Municipal College which had been built at a cost of £120,000. A unique experience of this mayoralty was that, being a widower, the Council installed his daughter Doris, aged five, as Mayoress — and she was a charming success. She raised £1,000 for the Children's Ward at the hospital, gave a birthday party to Crimean and Indian Mutiny veterans, and received the Duchess of Albany when she came to lay the foundation stone of a Wesleyan Sailors' and Soldiers' Home.

A Knight of Grace

1908

As the first Portsea Workhouse at the corner of Elm Road was more like a prison than a home for the destitute and dying, and was not far from the house in which Charles Dickens was born, it has been suggested that the great novelist had actually visited it and seen the conditions under which they lived. Although there is no foundation for this, there is no doubt whatever that his story of Oliver Twist stirred the public conscience and hastened the day of reform. In 1842 a modern building was erected in St Mary's Road, and a more humane system was gradually introduced, but when Dr. Charles Knott, a man with broad views and reforming zeal, was appointed Medical Superintendent, he found the system of nursing left much to be desired. So he prepared a plan for the training of nurses, with the hearty approval of the Guardians, and the result was so good that the plan came to be adopted by other Boards of Guardians throughout the country. The doctor well deserved the honour conferred upon him of the Order of St John of Jerusalem. His death this year was a public sorrow.

Wedding Bells

1909

Alderman A. Leon Emanuel, who died this year, made provision in his will for the payment of marriage dowries to poor young lovers, and for the yearly presentation of watches to the best boys and girls in the schools. He was Mayor in 1894, and the Mayoress had the distinction of switching on the electric light for Portsmouth.

A Dockyard Mystery

1913

On the night of December 20th, the Semaphore Tower in the Dockyard was mysteriously destroyed by fire and two of the night watchmen lost their lives. There were rumours that it was the work of German spies, but the most diligent search failed to discover evidence of this. When the Tower was rebuilt, the old Lion Gate was placed at its base.

The Great War

1914

When the world tumbled into the horror of war in 1914, it marked a historic watershed in more ways than one. For centuries, Portsmouth had sent its soldiers and sailors to the battlefield. This time, war reached into the heart of the city, with volunteers manning essential services and women filling the gaps left by fighting men. It also provided — on a lone occasion — a foretaste of aerial bombardment. On the night of September 25th, 1916, a single airship was reported off the South Coast and the people of Portsmouth were awakened by gunfire. In the huge sweeping beams of searchlights, they could clearly see a Zeppelin hastily gaining height to escape from the heavy anti-aircraft fire. A few bombs dropped harmlessly into the mud of the harbour, but this did not prevent the Chief of the German Naval Staff reporting two days later that "a section of our naval airships lavishly bombarded the British naval port of Portsmouth with explosives and incendiary bombs, with visible good results."

The Cenotaph

1921

The Cenotaph, described as "a thing of beauty and a mournful joy for ever," was unveiled on October 19th by the Duke of Connaught in the presence of a great assemblage. Although the money spent upon it might have been put to better use — as was the case at Gosport, where the memorial consisted of a new hospital of which the inhabitants are justly proud — the Cenotaph is a noble piece of work adjoining the Guildhall. Upon the panels at the back are inscribed the names of most of the men of Portsmouth who went forth never to return.

It has been estimated that Portsmouth lost about 6,000 men and women in the First World War. The Mayor's appeal raised £30,000 for the memorial, of which a third was devoted to the Royal Hospital. The unveiling drew a crowd estimated at 30,000. The British Legion's wreath was laid by former Sergeant J. Ockenden, V.C., M.M., and hundreds of other wreaths were laid, from huge official tributes to simple and touching family posies. Many people of Portsmouth felt it was a sad day when the Cenotaph was virtually hidden by the building of new Civic Offices and a public house.

A Priceless Heritage

1922

This year the City Council made the momentous decision to purchase Southsea Common from the War Office, with power to develop it eastward from a line drawn from the westward angle of Southsea Castle to the Grosvenor Hotel. The other portion had to be reserved as an open space so as to be available for military operations. The price paid for the historic ground was £45,000. To Mr. Leeke, the Lord of the Manor, the Corporation also had to pay £5,000. The Common was originally known as Froddington Heath, and was granted to the Abbey of Titchfield and sub-let to the Domus Dei. It later reverted to the Crown and was granted to the Leeke family.

The £5,000 paid to Mr. Leeke was to buy out the manorial rights which his family had kept when they sold the Common to the Government in 1785. In the First World War, part of it was dug up for use as allotments, and in the Second an anti-aircraft battery was stationed there.

The Old Gunwharf Transformed

1923

The decision of the Admiralty to transform the old Gunwharf into a training establishment for officers and men in torpedo warfare resulted in the birth of the shore-based H.M.S. Vernon in this year. Prior to this, the torpedo school comprised of three hulks in the harbour, one of which — H.M.S. Warrior — now occupies pride of place as a tourist attraction at a jetty on The Hard.

The Mills of Portsea Island

1923

The earliest of many mills on Portsea Island was built as early as 1212 near an entrance from the harbour to a great sheet of water which covered a large area of Portsea and became known as the Mill Pond. In 1714 one of the mills at Portsea was purchased by the Government, rebuilt and used for supplying food to the Forces until it was burned down in 1868. Towards the close of the 18th Century, when bread was very dear, the Dockyard shipwrights built a mill by the shore and it proved a blessing to the poor. In 1816 the Admiralty required the site, so the men built another in what was then Wish Lane, Southsea, and this remained until 1923. The last of the mills on the northern shore, known as Denison's, was burned down in 1863.

The picture shows Dock Mill, which was built off Albert Road and kept its distinctive sails until the turn of the century. With no one willing to buy it, the mill was demolished in 1923, but the adjoining Dock Mill Cottages remain to this day.

A Dream that came True

1924

To build a beautiful church in the midst of working class people was the lifelong ambition of the Rev. Bruce Cornford, and in this year his dream came true. It required £50,000 to build St Matthew's at Southsea, and then in 1941 the Germans destroyed the building in a night. The church was just off Fawcett Road, which at the beginning of the century was a country lane surrounded by orchards and known as Jews Lane because of the Jewish cemetery at the end of it. As an indication of public approval of Bruce Cornford's masterpiece, the collection at the opening ceremony was £1,175.

The Futcher Home of Recovery

1926

One of the most pleasing memories of the compiler of this panorama relates to a noble gift by Thomas Futcher, a Portsmouth bank manager. With four friends, who met by invitation at his charming little estate at Drayton, he astonished us by saying: "Look here, you fellows, my wife and I are just about to retire and have decided to transfer to you this property if you will agree to convert it into a convalescent home for afflicted children and provide us with a modest annuity." Of couse, we agreed with our whole hearts, and under the leadership of Sir John Rowland, also a loveable, generous soul, the annuity was provided, the estate transferred to us, and by us transferred to the Education Committee of the city, who rejoiced in being able to assist in such a good work. So the estate was converted into the Futcher Home of Recovery, a title chosen by the Board of Education, who gave the project a very warm blessing.

Sir John Rowland, a support of many deserving causes, was killed in an air disaster in 1933. It was mainly due to his enterprise and generosity that the Portsmouth section of the former Cripples' Hospital at Alton was established.

The Navy Honours its Dead

1924

The Naval Memorial of the Great War of 1914-18 on the Esplanade at Southsea bears the following inscription: "In honour of the Navy and to the abiding memory of those ranks and ratings who laid down their lives in defence of the Empire and have no other grave than the sea." It was unveiled by the Duke of York in October this year and dedicated to the 9,000 men killed in the First World War. In 1953, the Duke's widow — the present Queen Mother — unveiled an extension to it in the form of a sunken walled garden, dedicated to the fallen of the Second World War.

An Honour too Long Delayed

1926

This year Portsmouth was raised to the dignity of a city, and Councillor Frank Privett had the proud distinction of becoming its first Lord Mayor. It was an honour too long delayed, for outside London, there is no city or town in the realm more closely associated with international courtesies. In this respect it has always extended gracious hospitality to visiting monarchs, statesmen and ambassadors, none of whom could understand why a place of such importance was not designated a city.

Victory to Victory for ever

1928

In January, H.M.S. Victory was towed to her last berth in the Dockyard and embedded in cement on the site of the first dry dock in this country. Then came the happy idea: "Why not restore her to the condition in which she fought at Trafalgar?" On July 17th, King George V, himself a sailor, crowned the restoration by unveiling a plaque setting forth her glorious service for 175 years. At her masthead may still be seen the same red cross on a white field under which Hawkins and Blake fought, under which Myngs and Balchen perished, and under which the greatest seaman of them all received his death wound in one of the greatest naval battles of all time. We may see Nelson's cabin today as it was at Trafalgar. Here it was that he retired on the evening before the great fight to write his wonderful and immortal prayer for victory. In the cockpit close by, his life blood ebbed away as he strove to learn the result for which his soul had longed, which his clear brain had planned, and his mighty courage had inspired his captains to achieve. So

> "Victory to victory ever, hands the torch of
> glory on
> He is England's Admiral till setting of her sun."

Wyllie's Gift to the Nation

1931

The last work of Mr. W.L. Wyllie, the famous marine artist, was a panorama of the Battle of Trafalgar which he presented to the nation. When he died, the Navy paid him the unique honour of conveying his body up the Harbour to Portchester Castle in a cutter from H.M.S. Nelson, and the colours of the warships were dipped as the procession passed. It was through the Roman Water Gate at the castle that his body was carried to its resting place.

Lumps Fort

1931

As Lumps Fort, erected on the shore at Southsea in 1539, passed out of active service, the War Office sold it to the Corporation, with 13 acres of cultivated land, for £47,000. To the honour of the War Office, they refused a far higher offer from a syndicate who wanted it for development as a funfair. The Fort was subsequently converted into a particularly restful rose garden area.

Salute the Dying Day

1931

On the last day of September, the Evening Gun was fired for the last time in Portsmouth, to the regret of all who had any regard for ancient custom and picturesque ceremony. From time immemorial it had been the custom to fire a gun at sunset from the eastern end of the fortifications and lower the Union Jack, which had been flying throughout the day. At the same time, every ship in harbour saluted by bugle as the White Ensign came fluttering down. Portsmouth pleaded with the War Office for the restoration of this time-honoured custom, but the request was curtly refused and Brigadier Montgomery, when stationed at Portsmouth, also pleaded in vain.

Sir Walter Besant recorded the Evening Salute to the Sun as it was carried out in his day: "It was after eight; suddenly the sun, which a moment before was a great disc of burnished gold, sank below the thin line of land between sky and sea. Then the Evening Gun from the Duke of York's Bastion proclaimed the death of another day with a loud report which made the branches in the trees above us shake and tremble. And from the Barracks in the town, from the Harbour Admiral's Flagship, from the Port Admiral's Flagship, from the Flagship of the Admiral in command of the Mediterranean Fleet, then in harbour, from the tower of the old church, there came such a firing of muskets, such a beating of drums, playing of fifes and sounding of trumpets, that you would have thought the sun was setting once and for all and receiving his farewell salute from a world he was leaving for ever to roll about in darkness."

The Brigadier Montgomery referred to was, of course, the celebrated soldier who went on to become Field Marshal Viscount Montgomery of Alamein, Freeman of Portsmouth and a post-war President of Pompey Football Club.

A King Bids Portsmouth Farewell

1936

To the sorrow of the Commonwealth, King Edward VIII announced his "final irrevocable decision to renounce the Throne." Two hours later he travelled to Portsmouth through the darkness, embarked on a destroyer, and sailed for a new home overseas. As the first Freeman of the newly-formed City of Portsmouth, he did honour to the Navy which for a thousand years had found here its chief home.

Into the Blackout

1939

On the morning of Sunday, September 3rd, Britain's premier naval port found itself once more at war. A huge and complex scheme was begun to evacuate the city's children to safer areas of the surrounding countryside, but although thousands left by bus, train, and paddle steamer (for the Isle of Wight), many more stayed put. The authorities faced an uphill task persuading parents that their offspring would be better off away from their homes, especially when the widely expected bombing raids failed to materialise in the first months of the war. The picture was to change dramatically.

The First Bombs

1940

The evening of July 11th saw the beginning of the aerial terror which was to bedevil Portsmouth for years. Bombs claimed a number of civilian casualties and wrecked homes, shops and pubs. The German raiders were back on the morning of August 12, but saved their mass attack for the busy Saturday afternoon of August 24, when more than 60 bombs fell on Portsmouth, killing 117 people and causing widespread damage. After two smaller raids that month, things quietened down. It was a deceptive lull.

Terror from the Skies

1941

Portsmouths blackest night of the war was January 10th, when 300 enemy bombers made a concentrated attack, showering the city with incendiary bombs and high explosives. One of the first bombs scored a direct hit on the electricity generating station, plunging homes and shelters into darkness. Buildings tumbled and burned throughout the night, and the morning's scene of desolation was hard for the city to comprehend. Huge areas were in ruins, 171 people were dead, 430 injured, and 3,000 left homeless. Many historic buildings in Old Portsmouth had disappeared, and the heart of the city — the Guildhall — lay in smoking ruins.

The Great Invasion

1944

As preparations began for the Allied invasion of Northern France, the South of England found itself once more a target for Luftwaffe attacks in the spring of 1944 when hundreds of thousands of troops were crowding into the coastal area. The raiders met such a stiff anti-aircraft barrage, coupled with the furious fire of the rocket battery on Southsea Common, that most of their bombs were dropped either in the sea or the open countryside, and casualties were few. Once the momentous date of D-Day, June 6, had passed and the first troops had established a beach-head on the coast of Normandy, German prisoners-of-war began to arrive in Portsmouth and Gosport. The enemy's final fling was to send a rain of flying bombs, or "doodlebugs" as they were called, on to the South Coast. The last such bomb to fall on the city caused 15 deaths and scores of injuries, as well as widespread damage, in Newcomen Road, Stamshaw.

Peace at Last

1945

There were scenes of wild jubilation throughout the city when the German surrender was announced and May 8th was officially declared VE-Day — Victory in Europe. A crowd estimated at 25,000 filled Guildhall Square and despite an official ban on bonfires, a huge conflagration was started on to which were thrown trestles, air raid notice boards, gates, and seats from Victoria Park. The scene was repeated the following night, when a crowd burned the huge indicator board in front of the Guildhall which had shown the progress of war savings. Three months later, with victory over Japan assured, there were equally wild scenes, this time with pub doors and furniture carried away to fuel the bonfires. Thousands gathered around three official bonfires at Southsea Common, Portsdown Hill, and Great Salterns, while scores of smaller fires burned merrily on waste land and in side streets.

Healing the Scars

1946

The war-time bombing raids had left cruel scars across wide areas of Portsmouth, and housing was the city's most pressing need in the early days of peace. Army huts on Southsea Common provided temporary accommodation for more than 60 families, and 50 naval huts at the former Stockheath Camp at Havant were also brought into use as makeshift homes. In February, 1946, work began on the first permanent post-war homes with a development of 54 houses and two shops at Peterborough Road, Wymering. The cost was £59,054. Elsewhere in the city, strange new structures were appearing — factory-built units which became universally known as "prefabs." The first pair were opened at Paulsgrove in March this year, and the Evening News said of the two-storey steel-framed buildings: "Without being in any way pretentious, they are of neat and serviceable design."

Dreams in the Air

1946

One of the great dreams before and just after the Second World War was the development of Langstone Harbour as a huge national base for the giant flying boats which lumbered across the globe. The City Council and both M.P.s were keen to see the idea developed, but there was fierce competition from Southampton and the Admiralty was not keen on having civil aircraft near the country's premier port. Although a Government report recommended Langstone as the best of three possible sites, and the Minister of Civil Aviation himself seemed enthusiastic on a visit to the area, the decision went against it. The scheme faded away — and so, too, did the flying boats after a few brief years of glory.

The Big Freeze

1947

One of the worst winters in living memory combined with a fuel crisis to bring misery to millions. Blizzards from January until March gave way to gales and floods in April, leaving the country battered and wondering if peace could be as cruel as war. Emergency power cuts were introduced in February, and millions were idle as factories halted. Office staff and shop assistants worked by candlelight, street lamps were lit only at major junctions, and police toured Portsmouth to warn against the use of radios, lights, and electrical appliances during prohibited hours. Snow followed snow, and on February 8, it fell in the city for seven hours continuously. At one stage of the winter, temperatures were below freezing for 28 out of 30 days. One of the worst dates was February 21, when buses and cars became icebound on Portsdown Hill and people had to walk up to eight miles to get home. By contrast, that summer was a glorious one with the temperature reaching 91 degrees on one memorable day in August.

The Birth of Leigh Park

1947

A major post-war scheme was the detailed planning of the city's new overspill area at Leigh Park to relieve the desperate overcrowding problem on Portsea Island. The 1,700-acre estate at Havant had been bought by the City Council in 1944 for £122,465 and the plan was to provide 7,000 homes as soon as possible. Included in the original project were nine schools, sports grounds, a swimming pool, community centres, tennis courts, bowling greens, and public gardens. The realities of the age of austerity meant that not all came to fruition.

D-Day Remembered

1948

On June 6th, the fourth anniversary of D-Day, Field Marshal Montgomery was back in Portsmouth to unveil the D-Day memorial at Southsea in a ceremony which was broadcast by the B.B.C. to millions around the world. French soldiers and sailors joined U.S. Marines and British troops in a guard of honour for the guests, who included the Mayor and town council of Arromanches, the Normandy town on whose beaches the landings were made. The memorial itself consisted of a simple block of concrete, similar to the anti-invasion defences which littered the South Coast during the war. After unveiling it, Viscount Montgomery told the huge crowd: "Here in Portsmouth your battle scars are visible for all to see. When I looked at them today, I remembered with pride that I am a Freeman of your city and can share these scars with you. And I do share them, because it was in Portsmouth that I lost everything I possessed by enemy bombing in January, 1941." The Freedom ceremony had been carried out on July 26th, 1946, at South Parade Pier, the spot from which much of the D-Day invasion had been mounted.

Death of a Proud Veteran

1949

The world's oldest warship afloat, the wooden-walled frigate H.M.S. Implacable, was sent to an ignominious end by being scuttled in the Channel on December 2nd. Launched in 1800 as the French ship Duguay-Trouin, she had been captured by the British at Trafalgar after exchanging shots with Victory. Various restorations had been carried out over the years, but by 1949 her timbers were so rotten that the cost of saving her was put at a prohibitive £500,000. As she was towed out of Portsmouth Harbour, a band played the National Anthem and the Marseillaise while the ship's company of H.M.S. Victory stood to attention as her old foe passed. Nine and a half miles south-west of the Owers Lightship, explosive charges which had been placed in her hull were detonated and a bugler played the Last Post. With the White Ensign and the French Tricolour flying bravely side by side, Implacable slipped beneath the waves. The incident prompted one naval officer to observe: "It is the worst thing that the Navy has ever done. We ought to be able to look after our old friends better than that." Implacable's figurehead is now on display in the grounds of the National Maritime Museum at Greenwich, and valuable French carvings from the ship are in store there.

The Chimes Ring Out Again

1950

There was an emotional gathering in Guildhall Square on the evening of May 8, when the celebrated Pompey Chimes rang out once more from the tower of the ruined Guildhall. Apart from a couple of impromptu soundings during the war by sailors who climbed up among the bells, they had been silent since the night of January 10th, 1941, when the city's civic pride burned to the ground. The occasion of their restoration was described by the Lord Mayor (Alderman J. Privett) as "comparatively small but of great significance to the citizens." As the hour of 7 p.m. approached, four Royal Marines buglers high in the tower sounded Reveille, and then the chimes rang majestically while a crowd of 10,000 listened in silence. When the City Fire Brigade repeated the Chimes a short while later, however, "a typical Fratton Park cheer was raised."

Violent Harbour Explosions

1950

Unpleasant wartime memories were revived when the Portsmouth Harbour area was shaken by two huge explosions on the evening of July 14. Six lighters being loaded with ammunition at Bedenham Pier, the Royal Naval Armament Supply Depot at Gosport, blew up at intervals of 50 minutes, causing damage over a widespread area. Fortunately no one was hurt, but the pier was destroyed and ammunition stores near the waterfront badly damaged. Frantic and heroic efforts were made to save an ammunition train on the jetty and most of the 40 trucks were hauled away in time, only a few blowing up. Shop windows as far away as West Street, Fareham, were blown out by the blast and front doors at Portchester were torn off their hinges. A further threat was caused by unexploded shells and ammunition being blown over a wide area.

Churchill Joins the Freemen

1950

The city's long-cherished ambition was fulfilled on December 11, when Mr. Winston Churchill received the Freedom of Portsmouth from the war-time Lord Mayor, Sir Denis Daley. After being presented with a casket made from the oak of H.M.S. Victory, the former Prime Minister told guests: "This is an honour which I profoundly value and shall always cherish." Looking back over his long association with the city, he recalled the days between 1911 and 1914 when he had been in Portsmouth on most weekends to visit the Admiralty yacht Enchantress.

War Memorial Extended

1953

More than 16,000 relatives of naval personnel and a crowd of many thousands more watched the Queen Mother unveil the extension to the Naval War Memorial on Southsea Common in April. Made of Portland stone, it contained bronze panels which bore the names of 14,787 men and women killed during the Second World War. The Queen Mother, who had been widowed only the previous year, said: "I am especially proud to come as the wife of one who greatly loved the Royal Navy and all it stands for."

The Coronation Review

1953

Less than a fortnight after her Coronation, Queen Elizabeth II was in Portsmouth for a Fleet Review on June 15. The crowds were so dense when she arrived the previous evening that what was scheduled as a 13-minute drive from Portsdown Hill to the Dockyard took nearly three times as long. On several occasions the Royal car was brought to a standstill as enthusiastic well-wishers spilled into the road and surrounded it. At 3 a.m. on the morning after the Review, home-going traffic was reported to be still bumper-to-bumber on the outskirts of the city.

The Shape of the Future

1955

A massive scheme for reshaping the face of post-war Portsmouth was unveiled on December 2nd with a plan which looked 15 years into the future. It provided for the demolition of 7,000 properties and their replacement mainly with flats. Two-fifths of those whose homes were due to disappear were offered new homes at either Paulsgrove or Leigh Park. The areas mainly affected by the redevelopment were Portsea, Southsea, Stamshaw, and Landport.

The Russians Call In

1956

When the so-called Cold War was at its height, Portsmouth found itself playing host this year to the joint leaders of Russia, Marshal Nikolai Bulganin and Mr. Nikita Kruschev — or, as the popular Press inevitably dubbed them, B and K. They arrived on April 18th on board the huge modern cruiser Ordzhonikidze, accompanied by two Russian destroyers and watched by a mere handful of spectators on The Hard. Although the Lord Mayor and various officials were waiting at the Town Station, the two Russians exchanged only the briefest of courtesies before settling down in their special train, leaving the civic party shivering on the platform in a chilly April wind. Relations gradually improved during the ten-day visit, however, and by the time Russian sailors were giving a rousing chorus of "Tipperary" at a special concert on South Parade Pier, the atmosphere was positively convivial. An Evening News reporter did record that miniature searchlights "blazed from the stern of the three Soviet ships and lit up the water immediately astern." It was a telling comment, for during the visit a former naval diving expert, Commander "Buster" Crabbe, disappeared in mysterious circumstances in the harbour, amid speculation that he had been exploring the keel of the Russian cruiser. Although a headless body was later found off the coast, and was claimed to be that of Crabbe, the episode has never been satisfactorily or conclusively explained.

The Guildhall Reopens

1959

Using a pair of antique scissors to cut a white silk ribbon, the Queen brought Portsmouth's civic heart back to life on June 8th when she opened the newly restored Guildhall. Her Majesty told thousands who had waited in driving rain: "When my father and mother visited Portsmouth in 1941, your Guildhall, which my great-grandfather had opened, had been in ruins for less than a month. I am glad today to continue that deep interest which my family have always taken in your affairs by coming here to see this fine building that has risen from those ruins." That evening a crowd estimated at 20,000 gathered in Guildhall Square to join in community singing and watch the arrival of torchlight processions before ending with rousing choruses of Auld Lang Syne and the National Anthem. In a special commemorative issue, the Editor of the Evening News wrote: "The older generation of Portmuthians remember with pride what the Guildhall used to mean to them; the younger generation are about to find out."

The Vanguard Aground

1960

There was a last-minute drama as the 44,000-ton battleship H.M.S. Vanguard left Portsmouth for the breaker's yard on August 4th. She started to veer towards the Gosport shore, then corrected her swing but turned towards Point and ran aground in mud with her bows virtually touching the jetty by the Customs House. There she stayed for 45 minutes until ocean-going tugs were called in as reinforcements to help pull her clear. The huge ship had been laid down in 1941 and commissioned five years later. In 1947, she took the Royal Family to South Africa on the first visit ever paid to that country by a reigning monarch and his Queen.

Even the Sea Froze

1963

Langstone Harbour froze over for the first time in 60 years and ice up to four feet thick was recorded as 1963 shivered into being. Trains were halted, scores of minor roads in Hampshire blocked by drifts, and skiers on the Isle of Wight found themselves level with hedge tops. After a brief thaw, the Arctic conditions returned. There were increasing power cuts, Fareham Creek froze over, and on one day in January 20 Portsmouth schools were closed because of frozen toilets. When the main thaw did eventually come, several boats were carried out to sea still embedded in the ice, and were never seen again.

Enter the Tricorn

1966

As Portsmouth's reshaping continued, the controversial concrete development between Charlotte Street and Market Way was officially named the Tricorn in March this year. The complex of buildings, containing a car park, wholesale market, shops, warehouses and flats, won a Civic Trust award in 1966 but was voted the fourth ugliest structure in Britain in a poll of 500 designers the following year. Economic conditions were blamed for the traders' reluctance to move in, and within two years the City Council was on the verge of adapting a department store as the site for the new central library. The idea was eventually rejected on economic grounds, and the new library was built in the remodelled Guildhall Square.

The Fleet Air Arm's Day

1966

The Navy was out in force at Gosport on May 20th when the Freedom of the borough was conferred on the Fleet Air Arm. Eight hundred officers and ratings paraded through the streets with a 100-strong guard from H.M.S. Daedalus, and a formation of 28 aircraft flew over the harbour, led by a Fairey Swordfish, the legendary "Stringbag" of World War II. The Evening News commented: "Gosport, home of naval aviation since the hair-raising days of wood, glue and hope, rose to salute the Navy's striking arm."

Arise, Sir Alec

1967

All hearts were stirred by the achievement of a Southsea greengrocer called Alec Rose, who set off on July 16 to sail single-handed round the world in his small yacht, Lively Lady. The 59-year-old former naval lieutenant had started off on a similar attempt the previous year, but had run into a string of problems, including being run down in the Atlantic by an unidentified steamer. This time he was more fortunate, and when he stepped ashore in Australia in December, he was telephoned by the Lord Mayor of Portsmouth to be told that he was to be made a Freeman of his home city. He began his homeward voyage in January the following year, and on July 4th, 1968, a host of small and large craft welcomed this remarkable sailor home. The following day, it was announced that he was to be knighted, and on October 21st — Trafalgar Day — he received the Freedom of Portsmouth.

A Double Air Crash

1967

Portsmouth had the unenviable distinction of witnessing two air crashes in the same afternoon at the city's airport. The amazing sequence of events started when an Avro turboprop of Channel Airways crashed on landing in heavy rain on August 15. Fortunately the 21 passengers and four crew were only shaken, but while airport staff were still recovering from the shock, the second drama occurred. A similar aircraft of the same airline was making its second attempt to land when it veered off the runway and slewed through a boundary fence, coming to rest completely blocking Eastern Road. Again there were no injuries.

A City's Changing Face

1968

This year saw the beginning of one of the busiest building periods in the city's history. The ambitious scheme for redeveloping Guildhall Square began when the Lord Mayor (Councillor D.D. Connors) drove a mechanical excavator through the wall of the Greetham Street car park. The new Civic Offices, costing £8 million, were opened eight years later in all their black glass glory, and meant that staff who had been scattered around the city since the end of the war were at last all under one roof, although a few departments remained in the Guildhall. In the same year, the council accepted a tender of nearly £2,500,000 for what was to prove one of its most controversial undertakings, the massive Portsdown Park housing development. The Ministry of Transport also gave permission for the council to proceed with the Farlington by-pass section of the M27 between Portsbridge and the Broadmarsh roundabout at Havant.

The NATO Review

1969

More than 60 ships from 12 countries assembled at Spithead in May for a prestigious NATO Review, attended by the Queen, the Duke of Edinburgh, and Princess Anne.

The Marshes are Saved

1970

Amid fears that Farlington Marshes on the northern outskirts of the city might be sold at auction, the council bought the area for £43,500 under a compulsory purchase order. Three years later it was leased to the Hampshire and Isle of Wight Naturalists Trust as a nature reserve. On the other side of Portsea Island, the council sold 125 acres of reclaimed land at the northern end of the harbour to IBM as the site for a U.K. headquarters. The huge multi-national computer company had chosen Portsmouth from 22 locations in England which it had examined.

A Hovercraft Tragedy

1970

Five people died when a hovercraft overturned in rough seas as it was coming in to Southsea from Ryde. Those on the shore watched in horror as the 30-ton craft rose on its side and toppled over. Twenty two people survived the accident, clambering out of the submerged cabin as water flooded in and climbing on to the capsized hull to await rescue by helicopter. Experts said that a ten-million-to-one chance caused the tragedy, and the official inquiry concluded that it was due to an unusual combination of circumstances, with strong winds and a dangerous sea.

Disaster in the Channel

1970

A huge cloud of choking smoke rose like a funeral pall when a 42,000-ton supertanker exploded after colliding with another tanker off the Isle of Wight. Thirteen Chinese seamen died on board the Pacific Glory and others were critically injured as its cargo of crude oil was rocked by a series of blasts. The huge ship eventually went aground off Sandown after causing what Lloyd's Shipping described as "vast pollution." More than 200 Fire Service personnel were involved, as well as naval fire-fighters, and three firemen later received the British Empire Medal for courage and efficiency.

Trapped in a Submarine

1971

Three submariners were trapped for ten hours on the seabed when H.M.S. Artemis sank at her moorings at H.M.S. Dolphin, Gosport, on July 1st. Eight men had managed to leap to safety as the boat started to go down in 30 feet of water, but their companions faced a long and dark night during which they maintained radio contact with another submarine. Shortly after dawn, the trio surfaced from the escape hatch of Artemis. Two weeks later, they were among the first naval personnel to receive the newly-introduced submariners' metal badge, featuring two dolphins supporting a crown.

The Theatre Royal Blazes

1972

Crowds gathered outside the 116-year-old Theatre Royal when a fierce blaze broke out on October 28th. As flames ripped through the roof and interior, there were many who thought it would spell the end of hopes to preserve the historic home of drama in the city. The badly damaged shell survived, however, to be lovingly restored throughout the 1970s and 1980s. Part of it was reopened to the public as a restaurant in 1987.

Farewell to the Airport

1972

After a long and sometimes emotive debate, the City Council decided that the 40-year-old airport adjoining Eastern Road would close from the end of 1973. Although some councillors were convinced it still had a future, others described it as "this pocket handkerchief of an airfield" and "this wasteful grass landing strip." At one time it was suggested that Portsmouth Football Club might move in to the vacated area, but it was eventually redeveloped as a mixture of housing and industry.

The Growing City

1973

As pressure on land and demand for housing increased, Portsmouth continued its outward growth. On April 4th, the Housing Committee approved the final layout for a huge new overspill estate at Crookhorn Lane, Purbrook, providing 318 houses and 490 flats for more than 3,000 people.

A Stormy Start

1974

High tides and storm-force winds caused flooding on seafront roads at Southsea and Old Portsmouth in the first days of the new year. On the night of January 10th, 100 m.p.h. winds battered the Solent, Isle of Wight, and South Hampshire as freak storms swept across the country. The gale was so fierce that wind-recording instruments at The Needles went "off the clock" at 2 a.m. on January 11th. A 100 m.p.h. hurricane returned five days later, damaging more than 30 houses in Portsmouth and flattening commercial glasshouses at Titchfield. On February 10th, screaming winds were back so strongly that a Coastguard spokesman said: "It makes the Roaring Forties look like the Doldrums."

All Change in the Chamber

1974

Local government history was made on March 26th, when the City Council met for the last time as a county borough. There was a lengthy review of its achievements and a message of encouragement to its sister towns, Fareham and Havant, which had been raised to borough status under the reorganisation. Then the council concentrated on getting used to a new role in which it was responsible for housing, planning, environmental health, leisure, museums, arts, passenger transport and docks. Portsmouth had been one of 61 county boroughs established by the 1888 Local Government Act, and a commemorative scroll was presented to Councillor J.P.N. Brogden, Lord Mayor at the time of the historic change.

Birth of a Ferry Port

1975

Few people would have dared to forecast such a dramatic success for the city's new ferry port when the first lorry load of chalk was tipped into the sea to start work on August 4th, 1975. The following June, maiden voyages were made to Cherbourg and St Malo, and everyone was toasting a port which had been dubbed Portsmouth's 300-day wonder. Crowds in Guildhall Square celebrated the inaugural sailings with an evening of entertainment and open-air dancing, and the Evening News commented: "If this is to be the pattern, Portsmouth will at last be able to shrug aside the image of drabness and indecision that it has too often projected in the past." A year later, agreement was reached with Townsend-Thoresen to introduce a route to Le Havre, and within a few months Sealink had joined the other companies with a freight and passenger service to the Channel Islands. When an £8m. scheme got under way in 1983 to add a reclaimed six-acre peninsula for the use of Brittany Ferries, it was described as the most successful local government commercial enterprise in Portsmouth's history. The opening of the M275 motorway link to the very gates of the ferry port in 1976 had made Portsmouth an increasingly popular choice with motorists bound for the Continent.

A Tudor Time Capsule

1982

An historian's dream came true on the morning of October 10th, 1982, when the remains of Henry VIII's warship Mary Rose were raised from the waters of the Solent. The idea of salvaging the vessel had been a burning ambition since the day in 1967 when a sonar sounding being taken by author and historian Alexander McKee and his colleagues revealed the Tudor treasure. Slowly, the amazingly preserved timbers broke the surface of the waters which had hidden them for 437 years, and despite a heart-stopping moment when the cradle seemed about to collapse, Mary Rose was towed to safety at her new home in Portsmouth Dockyard. Archaeological Director Margaret Rule and her team oversaw the patient work of conserving the wealth of objects recovered from the seabed, and within a year the first paying visitors were gazing at the ship which had been the pride of the monarch who built the Royal Navy.

War in the Falklands

1982

In an atmosphere almost of disbelief, Portsmouth found itself once again preparing for war in the spring of 1982. Shortly before dawn on April 2, Argentine troops had invaded the Falkland Islands, the remote British territory in the South Atlantic to which they had laid claim for decades. After overpowering the tiny force of Royal Marines garrisoned there, the Argentines called up reinforcements and about 10,000 troops were dug in. The British response was swift, and within three days the first ships of a large naval task force, including the aircraft carriers Hermes and Invincible, were sailing from Portsmouth. The ten-week campaign which followed was a costly one, but a tribute to the courage and tenacity of the 25,000 men who fought a lonely war 8,000 miles from their homes. The price of victory was high: 250 soldiers, sailors, airmen, and merchant seamen were killed and seven naval vessels lost, as well as 20 aircraft. But by June 13, British troops were on the outskirts of Port Stanley, capital of the Falklands, and the following day the Argentines surrendered. As the ships came home to Portsmouth and Southampton, there were tumultous scenes of welcome not seen since the end of the Second World War. Among them were the luxury liners Queen Elizabeth II, Canberra and Uganda, pressed into service as troopships and hospital ships respectively. There was an especially warm reception for the carrier H.M.S. Hermes, flagship of the task force commander Rear-Admiral John Woodward (later, as Admiral Sir John Woodward, to become the Commander-in-Chief at Portsmouth).

To Botany Bay Once More

1987

Portsmouth's claim to be the birthplace of Australia was cemented in spectacular fashion on May 13th, when the Queen and the Duke of Edinburgh visited the city as part of a colourful programme of events to commemorate that country's bicentenary. Aborigine dancers entertained a huge crowd in Guildhall Square, marching bands provided stirring music, and the highlight of the day was a re-enactment of the departure of the first convict fleet, which sailed from Portsmouth on May 13th, 1787, to found a new continent. Modern square-rigged sailing vessels played the part of the original ships and re-created the eight-month voyage to Australia with the aim of arriving exactly 200 years to the day after their ancestors. To mark the link between the two countries, Her Majesty unveiled a commemorative plaque at Sallyport, Old Portsmouth, scene of many a historic departure.

The Warrior Returns

1987

Crowds lined the shore on the afternoon of June 16th to watch the triumphal return of H.M.S. Warrior, the Royal Navy's first ironclad, which had been based at Portsmouth for most of her life. Launched in 1860, the magnificent 9,000-ton vessel had been the pride of the Victorian Navy with her massive armament and revolutionary defensive armour plating. Her later career had been undistinguished, first as a torpedo training hulk in Portsmouth Harbour and later as a floating jetty for oil ships at Milford Haven. Rescued in 1979, she was towed to Hartlepool for a £7,000,000 restoration programme from which she emerged in her original glory. She returned to her home port, and a permanent berth at The Hard, as a unique tourist attraction.

RECCE
59
COMMANDO R.E
RULE
BRITANNIA
STRIKE
WELL CALL
STRIKE!
SQUADRON
ENGINEERS
MED
CANBERRA
LONDON

Index

CONSECRATED
LORD VISCOUNT NELSO
TRAFALGAR
MDCCCV